VISUAL STUDIO CODE

Visual Studio Code

END-TO-END EDITING AND DEBUGGING
TOOLS FOR WEB DEVELOPERS

Bruce Johnson

WILEY

Visual Studio Code: End-to-End Editing and Debugging Tools for Web Developers

Published by
John Wiley & Sons, Inc.
10475 Crosspoint Boulevard
Indianapolis, IN 46256
www.wiley.com

ISBN: 978-1-119-58818-4
ISBN: 978-1-119-58830-6 (ebk)
ISBN: 978-1-119-58821-4 (ebk)

Manufactured in the United States of America

For general information on our other products and services please contact our Customer Care Department within the United States at (877) 762-2974, outside the United States at (317) 572-3993 or fax (317) 572-4002.

Wiley publishes in a variety of print and electronic formats and by print-on-demand. Some material included with standard print versions of this book may not be included in e-books or in print-on-demand. If this book refers to media such as a CD or DVD that is not included in the version you purchased, you may download this material at http://booksupport .wiley.com. For more information about Wiley products, visit www.wiley.com.

Library of Congress Control Number: 2019944259

C10012794_080619

ABOUT THE AUTHOR

BRUCE JOHNSON is a partner at ObjectSharp Consulting and has been working in the computer industry for 33 years (has it really been that long?). During that time, he has gone from writing UNIX code for mainframes and minicomputers to focusing on PCs and Windows. It was really the advent of Visual Basic and the World Wide Web in the early 1990s that triggered that change. But since then, he has been working on projects that are at whatever the leading edge of Windows technology happened to be. This means he has built rich client applications, web applications, services, and APIs. And there has been a sprinkling of database and front-end development thrown in for good measure. Just because.

As well as having fun with building systems, Bruce has spoken hundreds of times at conferences and user groups throughout North America. He has been a Microsoft Certified Trainer (MCT) and the co-president of the Metro Toronto .NET User Group. He has also written columns and articles for numerous magazines. For all this activity, Bruce was also a Microsoft MVP for more than ten years. At the moment, he's already working on the outline for his next book.

ABOUT THE TECHNICAL EDITOR

BENJAMIN PERKINS is currently employed at Microsoft in Munich, Germany, as a Senior Escalation Engineer for IIS, ASP.NET, and Azure App Services. He has been working professionally in the IT industry for over two decades. He started computer programming with QBasic at the age of 11 on an Atari 1200XL desktop computer. He takes pleasure in the challenges that troubleshooting technical issues has to offer and savors the rewards of a well-written program. After completing high school, he joined the United States Army. After successfully completing his military service, he attended Texas A&M University in College Station, Texas, where he received a Bachelor of Business Administration in Management Information Systems. He also received a Master of Business Administration from the European University.

ACKNOWLEDGMENTS

I'D LIKE TO THANK MY four children, Curtis, Gillian, Cameron, and Kyle, for their love and support. They are teenagers or young adults now, so getting time alone to write wasn't a challenge. In fact, it was a regular request of theirs. But they have always been supportive of my writing projects and I am incredibly proud of them. My life would be much less rich without them.

My children are not the only people in my life who have been supportive of my writing. There is one other, whose modesty and desire for privacy prevents me from acknowledging them by name, who has been a large part of my impetus to write, not just this book but others. They know who they are and how grateful I am for their support.

Writing a book is a strange combination of lonely and collaborative. Much of the text is written while sitting late at night at a desk or on weekend mornings in a coffee shop. But once the first draft is complete, it gets passed into the hands of some incredibly talented people. And those people are the reason why the prose is grammatically correct, in the active voice, and flows in a logical sequence. It has always been a pleasure to work with the editors, technical editors, and copy editors of Wiley, and this book was no exception. I'm incredibly grateful for their help and attention to detail. They are a big reason why you can read what I have written.

CONTENTS

INTRODUCTION

In a surprisingly short period of time, Visual Studio Code has become very popular among web developers. Part of that is because it's fast, lightweight, and is available on the three main platforms (Windows, Mac, Linux). But it also boasts several features that set it apart from the competition. This includes support for IntelliSense, refactoring capabilities, and an extensive ecosystem of extensions. But even beyond the features that help developers craft code, there is also debugging support. It's possible to open a .NET Core project from within Visual Studio Code and get end-to-end execution and debugging functionality.

The goal of this book is to help developers become not just familiar, but productive in Visual Studio Code. It starts with an introduction to the editing features of the workspace and continues with the more advanced functionality (including refactoring and key bindings). The book finishes with an extensive look at the extensibility of Visual Studio Code, so that you can add whatever functionality you need to make you days more productive.

WHAT DOES THIS BOOK COVER?

Here is a glance at what's in each chapter.

Chapter 1: Introducing Visual Studio Code introduces the cross-platform nature of the tool, along with the steps to install Visual Studio Code on Windows, Mac, and Linux platforms.

Chapter 2: Exploring the User Interface examines the focal point of the development experience: the workspace. This chapter introduces the developer to the features of the workspace and how those features can be customized.

Chapter 3: Files and Folders and Projects (Oh My) considers the fluid structure of a web project. Visual Studio Code allows developers to choose the structure according to their needs. This chapter looks at the different ways Visual Studio Code supports the most common structures.

Chapter 4: Editing Code in Your Language of Choice discusses the Visual Studio Code editor. The editor is the heart of the developer experience and probably the most important chapter in the book. It covers syntax coloring, IntelliSense, refactoring, and code navigation.

Chapter 5: Integrating with Source Control covers the support that Visual Studio Code provides for source control, through both the Git integration that is available out of the box as well as third-party extensions for other source control providers. In this chapter, we look at how to perform common Git functions (commits, checkouts, branches, and merges) from within Visual Studio Code.

Chapter 6: Debugging Code looks at the support that Visual Studio Code has for many of the debugging features to which .NET developers have become accustomed. This chapter covers how to debug your code in both .NET Core and Node.js.

Chapter 7: External Tools and Task Automation describes Visual Studio Code's extensive capability to integrate with these tools and provides an environment in which the tasks associated with the tools can be automated.

Chapter 8: Unit Testing examines the support provided by Visual Studio Code for writing unit tests against your code. This chapter covers the unit testing capabilities in JavaScript and Python.

Chapter 9: Working with Extensions looks at the extensibility that is a big part of Visual Studio Code. Many extensions are available in the marketplace, from additional language support to tools that provide incredibly useful features. This chapter covers the options available to install and configure extensions and provides a description of the extensions that add the sort of functionality that developers live to discover.

Chapter 10: Creating Your Own Extensions covers how developers can create any additional tools that they need. This includes support for languages that might not already be included and features that can't be found in the marketplace. This chapter looks at how to extend Visual Studio Code to provide the functions that the developer needs.

WHO SHOULD READ THIS BOOK

The goal of the book is to provide the information needed by an existing web developer to be able to use Visual Studio Code to do full-stack development. The book remains agnostic on the language being used to develop the web application, although the examples are done in JavaScript, with occasional snippets of C# and Python.

I am making certain assumptions regarding the reader here:

➤   You are familiar with web technologies.

➤   You have a rudimentary understanding of editing and running code for web applications.

➤   You are aware of some of the concepts of source control providers, such as Git.

In general, I expect that most of the readers of this book will be existing developers who are intrigued by what they have heard about Visual Studio Code. For that group, the purpose of the book is to provide a basis for using the tool to do their development tasks. However, it's not like current Visual Studio Code users are ignored. For them, the goal of the book is to expand their knowledge of how the tool works and the extensions that are available. Regardless of which group a reader falls into, lots of information will be immediately useful and ultimately invaluable.

HOW TO CONTACT THE AUTHOR

We welcome your comments and questions! If you think you've found a mistake in the book, please tell us at errata@wiley.com. You can download the companion files that accompany each chapter from www.wiley.com/go/visualstudiocode and for any feedback you have about this project, you can contact me any of these ways:

@LACanuck

bjohnson@objectsharp.com

1

Introducing Visual Studio Code

WHAT'S IN THIS CHAPTER?

➤   Installing and getting started with Visual Studio Code

➤   Understanding the cross-platform components that make up Visual Studio Code

GETTING STARTED

The choice of the editor used by any developer is an incredibly personal one. The reason to pick one over the rest depends on a collection of attributes typically related to the tasks they perform on a daily basis. Developers look for functionality, keystroke shortcuts, code snippets, colorations, and more that allow them to stay productive.

Dislodging developers from their choice is not easy. Any change in editors is going to result in an immediate loss of productivity. After all, it takes time to become familiar with the features offered and have them become a natural part of the coding "flow." As a result, it takes a special level of "better" for a developer to switch editors.

For this reason, the success of Visual Studio Code speaks volumes for its features and functionality. Although it has been officially released for just three years (it left public preview in April 2016), it has quickly become one of the top editors in terms of popularity, competing with Sublime Text, Atom, and UltraEdit for the top spot.

But that doesn't matter to you, the reader. What you care about more is what Visual Studio Code can do to help you be productive. As a developer, it is frequently the small things that make the biggest difference—knowing how to add code with a single keyboard chord, being able to do client and server debugging on your Node.js project, or language-sensitive code completion. Any, all, or none of those might matter, but the goal of this book is to help you find the five or ten features that matter to you and that will make you excited to use Visual Studio Code.

Installing Visual Studio Code

Visual Studio Code is a cross-platform editor. In this instance, cross-platform means that a version is available to run on Windows (7, 8, and 10), macOS, and Linux. The installation process is similar for each, and the starting point is the same in all cases: `https://code.visualstudio.com/Download`. Figure 1-1 shows what the download page looks like presently, but it's naturally subject to change.

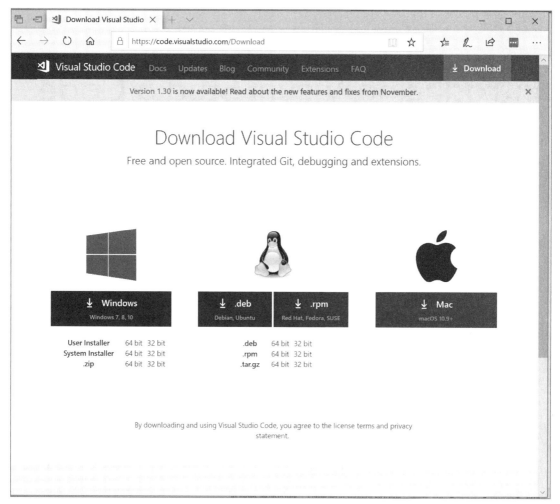

FIGURE 1-1

Windows

The most efficient starting point for a Windows installation is to download the desired installer. You have six possible options—three different installers each of which is available in 32-bit and 64-bit formats, divided along two separate attributes. First, you can choose from three installer types—System, User, and Zip:

➤ *System Installer*—This was the original installer for Visual Studio Code. It requires local Administrator privileges and places the executable and supporting files in the Program Files directory structure.

➤ *User Installer*—A more recent addition to Visual Studio Code, this installer does not require Administrator permission to be successful. Instead of placing the files into the Program Files structure, you can find the files in `AppData\Local\Programs` in your user directory. Because this is actually the preferred installer, you will be asked if you want to uninstall any versions that had been installed using the System Installer.

When Visual Studio Code is installed using one of these two installers, you will automatically be notified when an update is available. The pace of change for Visual Studio Code means that updates are delivered approximately once a month.

➤ *Zip*—The Zip option is just a ZIP compressed file containing the contents that are placed into `AppData\Local\Programs` by the User Installer. Once you have opened the file, you can copy the contents to whatever location you prefer. However, you're responsible for creating any links to the executable (called `code.exe`) that you want to place on your desktop or task bar. Also, you won't automatically receive updates. If you wish to use a more recent version, you'll need to download a new ZIP file and copy the files over again.

The second attribute available for the installer has a value of either 32-bit or 64-bit. This refers to the width of the data units supported by the CPU on your device. If you are running 32-bit Windows, choose the 32-bit version of the desired installer. If you are running 64-bit Windows, you can choose either the 32-bit or 64-bit version.

> **NOTE** *It will come as a disappointment to some, but this option does* not *mean that Visual Studio Code is a 64-bit application. It's not. Visual Studio Code is a 32-bit application regardless of whether or not it's running on a 64-bit version of Windows.*

For both the System and User Installers, running the installation program provides a similar experience. The following screens make up the installation process:

➤ *Welcome Screen*—Describes what you're about to do (that being, installing Visual Studio Code). The description indicates whether you are using the User or System Installer.

➤ *License Agreement*—The license agreement for Visual Studio Code is presented. You must accept the agreement before you can install the software.

➤ *Select Destination Location*—In this screen, shown in Figure 1-2, you choose the directory into which Visual Studio Code will be installed. The default is different for the User and System versions. For the User installation, it is placed in `C:\Users\<your username>\AppData\Local\Programs\Microsoft VS Code`. For the System installation, it is placed in `C:\Program Files (386)\Microsoft VS Code`. The (386) part of the directory is left off if you're running on a 32-bit operating system.

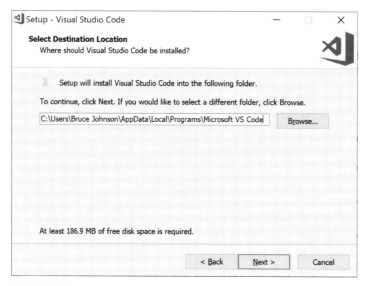

FIGURE 1-2

➤ *Select Start Menu Folder*—Once you have specified where Visual Studio Code will be installed, you get to identify where the links to the application are placed within your Start menu. The dialog to do this is shown in Figure 1-3. The default folder is Visual Studio Code, but you can provide another name, browse within your existing Start menu folders, or create a new one if you prefer. If you don't want to have any Start menu items added, check the Don't Create A Start Menu Folder checkbox at the bottom left of the dialog.

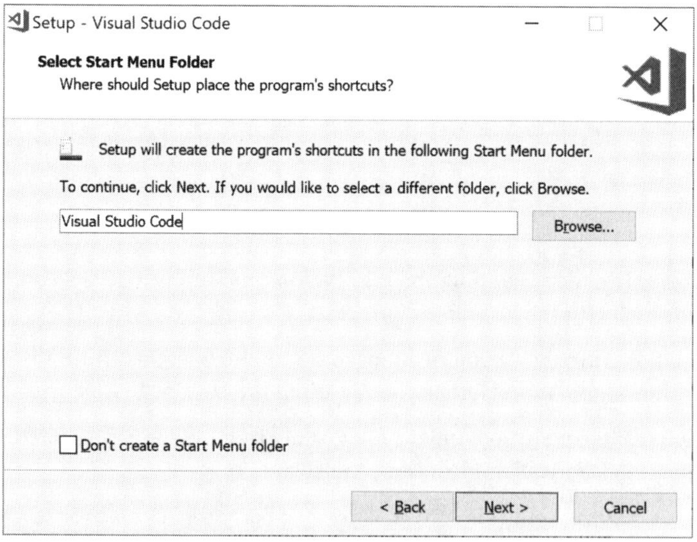

FIGURE 1-3

➤ *Select Additional Tasks*—A number of additional tasks can be performed as part of the installation process. The choices, available on the dialog shown in Figure 1-4, include:

  ➤ Creating a desktop icon that launches Visual Studio Code.

  ➤ Adding an Open With Code option to the context menu for Windows Explorer files and directories.

  ➤ Registering Visual Studio Code as an editor for any supported file types. This causes Visual Studio Code to appear in the Open With list of options in the context menu in Windows Explorer.

  ➤ Add the installation directory for Visual Studio Code to the PATH environment variable. This allows Visual Studio Code commands to be invoked from within a command-line tool. Keep in mind that it takes a restart of your computer for any changes to PATH to take effect.

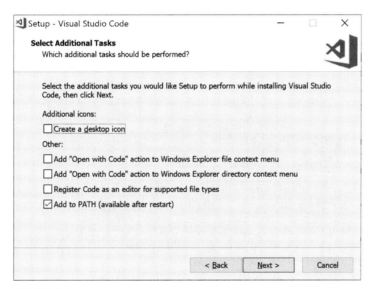

FIGURE 1-4

➤ *Ready To Install*—The final step in the installation process, as shown in Figure 1-5, is a summary of the options that you selected on the other screens. If you click Install, the installation commences.

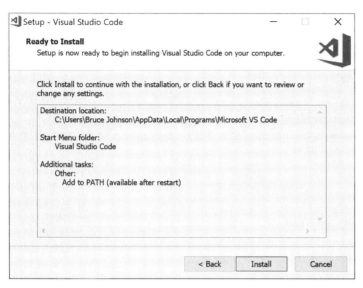

FIGURE 1-5

Linux

The basic steps involved with installing Visual Studio Code on Linux are the same regardless of the distribution you are using:

1. Download the appropriate software package.

2. Install it using the tools appropriate for your distribution.

However, the specifics within each of these steps do depend on your distribution. The precise instructions for a number of different distributions are described in the following sections.

All of the figures in this section were captured from within Ubuntu, so you might see something slightly different in your own environment. Also, be aware that you need to have a desktop installed in your Linux environment in order to run Visual Studio Code.

Ubuntu and Debian Distributions

The installation flow for Ubuntu or Debian is quite similar to Windows or macOS:

1. Open your favorite browser and navigate to `https://code.visualstudio.com/download`. Figure 1-6 shows what this web page looks like.

2. Identify the desired installation package and download it. 64-bit and 32-bit versions of Visual Studio Code are available, as well as a gzipped TAR file. Use the version suitable for your platform (that is, not the TAR file).

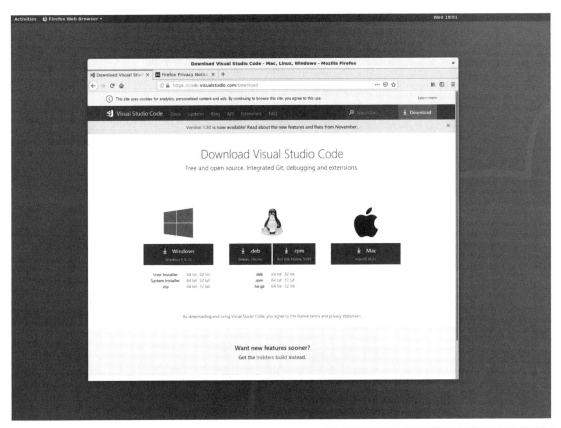

FIGURE 1-6

3. You will be prompted for what to do with the file. The dialog is shown in Figure 1-7. Though it might seem like opening with Software Install is the obvious choice, instead select the Save File radio button and click OK.

4. Once the file has been downloaded, open a Terminal window. Change the directory to the location where the file was downloaded. By default, the command to do this is:

FIGURE 1-7

```
cd ~/Downloads
```

5. Install the package using the apt utility:

```
sudo apt install ./<file>.deb
```

> **NOTE** *In some cases, it might be necessary to install some additional dependencies. If that happens, you will see the missing dependencies in the output from that last command. You can install the dependencies manually (using the same* apt install *command), or you can execute the following command to install all of the missing dependencies:*
>
> sudo apt-get install -f

At this point, Visual Studio Code should be ready to go. Execute `code` from within Terminal to launch the application (see Figure 1-8).

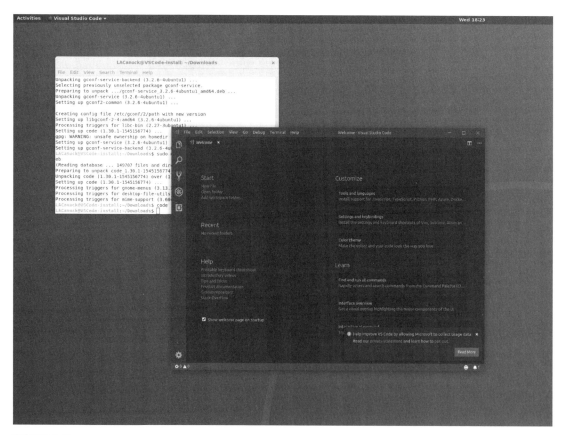

FIGURE 1-8

CentOS, Fedora, and RHEL Distributions

Another way to get the installation files for Visual Studio Code is through a YUM repository. Microsoft maintains a YUM repository that contains the current stable 64-bit version of Visual Studio Code.

> **NOTE** *A YUM (Yellowdog Updater, Modified) repository is a storehouse of RPM (Red Hat Package Manager) files. The purpose of the repository is to provide a simple mechanism through which software can be installed, dependencies resolved, and updates delivered. It's conceptually the same as NuGet or NPM (Node Package Manager).*

To install the key and the YUM repository, execute the following commands on your Linux machine:

```
sudo rpm --import https://packages.microsoft.com/keys/microsoft.asc
sudo sh -c 'echo -e "[code]\nname=Visual Studio
Code\nbaseurl=https://packages.microsoft.com/yumrepos/vscode\nenabled=1\
ngpgcheck=1\ngpgkey=https://packages.microsoft.com/keys/microsoft.asc" >
/etc/yum.repos.d/vscode.repo'
```

The first command imports the key to the repository into your environment. The second adds the Microsoft repository as a recognized YUM repository. This is accomplished by creating a file (called `vscode.repo`) and putting it in the `/etc/yum.repos.d` directory.

Once this is done, you can update the YUM package cache by executing the following command:

```
yum check-update
```

Now you're ready to actually install Visual Studio Code. The `yum install` command initiates the installation:

```
sudo yum install code
```

When the command is finished, Visual Studio Code is ready to run.

> **NOTE** *Microsoft uses a manual signing process for the package placed in the YUM repository. As a result, the system that is used to publish Visual Studio Code is not able to deliver an updated package at the same time as it is delivered to other distribution points (like the Visual Studio Code website); there might be a delay between updates being available on other platforms and in the YUM repository.*

OpenSUSE and SLE Distributions

For these distributions, the YUM repository is the best choice for getting Visual Studio Code. What differs are the commands that need to be executed. The following commands install the key and repository:

```
sudo rpm --import https://packages.microsoft.com/keys/microsoft.asc
sudo sh -c 'echo -e "[code]\nname=Visual Studio
Code\nbaseurl=https://packages.microsoft.com/yumrepos/vscode\nenabled=1\ntype=r-
pm-md\ngpgcheck=1\ngpgkey=https://packages.microsoft.com/keys/microsoft.asc" >
/etc/zypp/repos.d/vscode.repo'
```

These next two commands will update the package cache and install Visual Studio Code:

```
sudo zypper refresh
sudo zypper install code
```

Nix Package Manager

Another package manager that is occasionally found in the Linux world is Nix. Although Microsoft doesn't maintain a Nix package, a community-managed version is available at `https://github.com/NixOS/nixpkgs/blob/master/pkgs/applications/editors/vscode/vscode.nix`.

To install Visual Studio Code using Nix, set the `allowUnfree` option in your `config.nix` file to true. Then execute the following command:

```
nix-env -i vscode
```

macOS

The starting point for installing Visual Studio Code on macOS is, like Windows, the Visual Studio Code download page (found at `https://code.visualstudio.com/Download` and shown on Safari in Figure 1-9).

FIGURE 1-9

Click the Mac option on the right-hand side to start the download. When it has finished, open the download section on your browser and open the downloaded file. You will be greeted with a warning message indicating that the file you're trying to open came from the Internet (Figure 1-10).

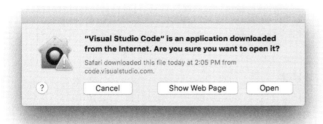

FIGURE 1-10

Click the Open button to expand the downloaded file. Because the download is a ZIP file, this means that the contents become visible. Drag the Visual Studio `Code.app` file to the `Applications` folder. This makes Visual Studio Code available in your Launchpad.

If you want to add Visual Studio Code to your dock, right-click the icon and choose Options ➤ Keep In Dock (Figure 1-11).

FIGURE 1-11

> **NOTE** *If you upgrade to macOS Mojave after installing Visual Studio Code, it's possible that you might start seeing dialogs suggesting that Visual Studio Code needs to access some common file locations. Specifically, you might see any or all of calendar, photos, and contacts in the dialog. These dialogs were a security addition to Mojave and, as such, are not specific to Visual Studio Code. Running other applications might generate the same dialogs. You are safe to answer Don't Allow to these requests. There is no need for Visual Studio Code to access these folders and there will be no impact on any functionality if you deny the request.*

How Cross-Platform Works

Although it is not essential to being able to use Visual Studio Code, it is instructive to understand the underpinnings that allow it to work across the disparate platforms that it supports. That is especially true if you have any thoughts about trying to create extensions for Visual Studio Code, a topic that is covered in Chapter 10, "Creating Your Own Extensions."

First, Visual Studio Code is an open-source project. This means that the source code is readily available for anyone to look at. Or even contribute to, if you have the desire. You can find the source at `https://github.com/Microsoft/vscode`.

Visual Studio Code is based on a framework called Electron. Electron was designed to allow for the creation of desktop applications using the front- and backend components of a web application. On the frontend side, JavaScript, HTML, and CSS are used to create the user interface functionality. The interface is rendered using Chromium.

> **NOTE** *Chromium is an open-source web browser project that is headed by Google. It is the foundation on which Chrome is built and will also be the basis for future versions of Microsoft's Edge.*

On the backend, Node.js is used to serve the user interface component and provide any additional functionality. This combination of technologies allows it to run on the desktop of three major platforms: Windows, macOS, and Linux.

Electron was originally created by GitHub and, ostensibly, its primary purpose was to support the Atom text editor. But its usage didn't stop there. It is currently used in a wide variety of applications, ranging from integrated development environments (IDEs) to music players to games.

Though Electron is the foundation on which Atom was built, Visual Studio Code does not use Atom as its editor. Instead, it uses the same text editor that is found in Azure DevOps (formerly named Visual Studio Team Services, which was formerly Visual Studio Online). The text editor is called Monaco. It is also open-source and available separately from Visual Studio Code (you can find the repository at `https://microsoft.github.io/monaco-editor`).

Additional common functionality is implemented through a number of other channels. For example, colorization is provided through Monarch, a library that allows you to specify a syntax highlighter using a declarative syntax. What's even better is that the syntax is expressed using JSON, something that is likely to be familiar to most web developers.

As another example, language-specific functionality, like auto-completion, formatting, and diagnostics, are implemented in a separate language server. This server runs in a process separate from Visual Studio Code, the goal being to minimize any impact on the IDE that performing continual lexographical analysis could have. Visual Studio Code communicates with these servers (there is typically one for each language you are editing) using the Language Server Protocol (LSP).

SUMMARY

You've seen how to install Visual Studio Code on the different operating systems that it supports. Once the application is ready, the user experience is very consistent across the platforms. That has to do with how Visual Studio Code was built (that is, on the Electron platform).

In subsequent chapters, you'll learn how to customize the IDE to more closely fit your own working style. You'll also see how Visual Studio Code works hard to make your development process easier and faster.

2

Exploring the User Interface

WHAT'S IN THIS CHAPTER?

➤ Exploring the different areas of the Visual Studio Code development environment

➤ Understanding the different windows that are available within Visual Studio Code

The key to being exceptionally productive in any development tool is being intimately familiar with the user interface, for the simple reason that the basic user interface will be the environment in which you spend the vast majority of your editing time. Yes, the quick key bindings are useful to know, as are the customizations and extensions that are available. But to be truly efficient in Visual Studio Code, you need to know the basic elements of the user interface and how they work together.

Figure 2-1 shows Visual Studio Code with a simple React app open.

> **NOTE** *The React App was creating using the* aspnetcore *command and the* react-redux *template, which is why you see the Controllers folder and the C# code.*

The basic user interface consists of four main areas, each marked in Figure 2-1 with a different letter:

➤ *Activity Bar* (labeled "A")—Located on the left side of the screen, the Activity Bar provides a mechanism to switch between different views.

➤ *Editors* (labeled "B")—This area contains the different editors that are open with Visual Studio Code. Each tab represents a different file, but it is possible to work on multiple files simultaneously, using a side-by-side or an above-and-below view.

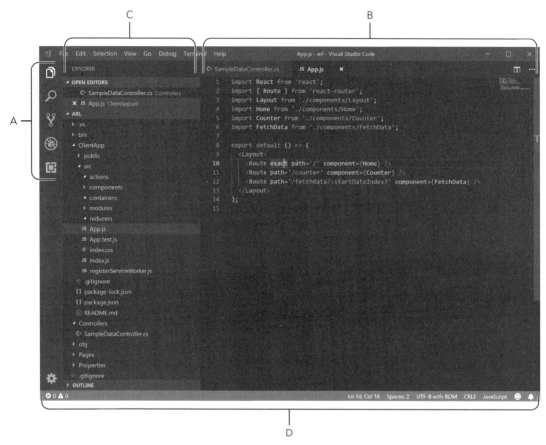

FIGURE 2-1

➤ *Side Bar* (labeled "C")—Contains different views of the workspace, such as the Explorer shown in Figure 2-1. It also acts as the launching point for working with source control, debugging your application, and interacting with any extensions you have installed.

➤ *Status Bar* (labeled "D")—Displays information about the current active workspace and the files that are being edited.

EDITORS

Because Visual Studio Code is, at its heart, a text editor (even granting the additional functionality provided), it seems reasonable to start in that area.

The area reserved for the different editors takes up the bulk of the application's surface. It's on the right-hand side of Figure 2-1 and the size at the top is indicated with the letter "B." This space is where the editors for all the different files you open appear.

The details of how to work with editors, lay out different editors to fit your need, and the many different features that are available are covered in Chapter 4, "Editing Code in Your Language of Choice."

ACTIVITY BAR

On the left side (by default) of Visual Studio Code is the Activity Bar. It is the area marked "A" in Figure 2-1 and can be seen in more detail in Figure 2-2.

The icons are each used to access a pane that contains information useful to the editing and developing process. Six icons are available. The first five, starting from the top, are Explorer, Search, Source Control, Debug, and Extensions. At the bottom is an icon that is used to access the settings for Visual Studio Code.

Each of these different icons is used to access parts of Visual Studio Code that are important enough and full-featured enough to warrant coverage in their own chapter. Explorer and Search are covered in Chapter 3, "Files and Folders and Projects (Oh My)." Source Control is covered in Chapter 5, "Integrating with Source Control." The Debug options are discussed in Chapter 6, "Debugging Code," and the installation and use of extensions are detailed in Chapter 9, "Working with Extensions."

The Settings icon is one of a couple ways to access the settings for Visual Studio Code. Clicking the icon displays a context menu, as shown in Figure 2-3.

Clicking the Settings option (highlighted in Figure 2-3) opens the Settings editor (Figure 2-4).

FIGURE 2-2

It's also possible to get to the Settings editor by using the File ⇨ Preferences ⇨ Settings menu option, or by using the Command Palette (View ⇨ Command Palette) and entering **Preferences: Edit User Settings**.

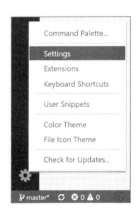

Settings are scoped into two separate blocks: user settings and workspace settings. You can see these two scopes as tab headers immediately below the Search Settings text box. The list of possible settings is mostly the same for each scope. The difference then becomes where the settings are persisted, and which one takes precedence.

User settings are applied to any instance of Visual Studio Code that you open. Exactly where the user settings are stored depends on your platform. For Windows, the file is located at `%APPDATA%\Code\User\settings.json`. For macOS, the location is `$HOME/Library/Application Support/Code/User/settings.json`. And for Linux, the settings are at `$HOME/.config/Code/User/settings.json`.

FIGURE 2-3

Workplace settings are applied to the specific workspace that is being opened. This means that the settings (also in a `settings.json` file) are stored in the same folder as the workspace. This makes it easier for settings to be shared between team members by simply moving the settings along with the rest of the files and folders.

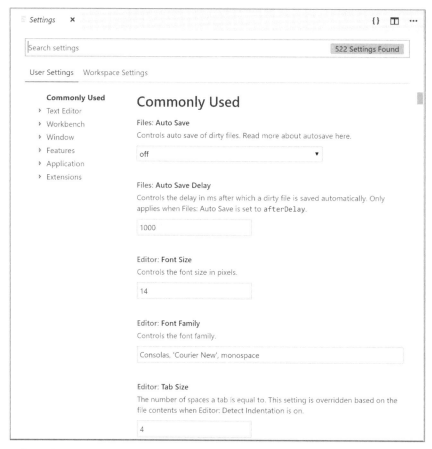

FIGURE 2-4

For the scope of the two groups of settings to be consistent with these definitions, any configuration value in the workplace settings overrides the same configuration in the user settings.

The settings are divided into a number of different categories. These categories appear in a tree navigation control on the left side of the Settings editor. Expanding any one of the categories displays a number of subcategories. When either a category or a subcategory is selected, the settings for that group are displayed at the right.

As well, and differently than many tree-like navigations, you can move between different groups of settings by using the scroll bar on the right. As you scroll up and down, the category and subcategory on the left will change, so you can actually scroll through all of the setting items without going through the categories.

As a last navigation function through the settings, there is a Search Settings text box at the top of the Settings editor. As you type into the text box, the settings that match your text appear in the rest of the editor. See Figure 2-5 for an example of entering **Exc** into the text box.

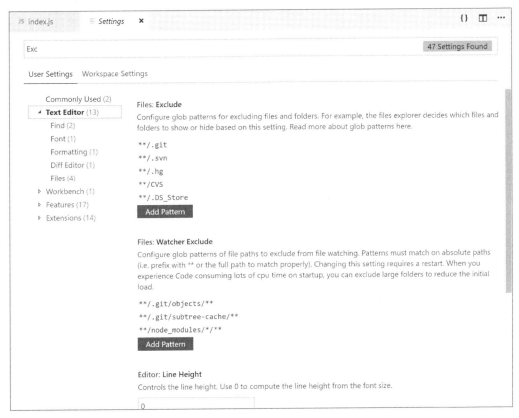

FIGURE 2-5

Notice that not only does the list of settings change based on the value in the text box, but so does the content of the categories on the left. If you expand the categories, you can see the number of settings in each of the categories that match the filter value.

Editing Settings Manually

Visual Studio Code provides two ways to edit settings. The first is through the user interface that was just described. But you can also edit the settings manually, and, for some of the settings, manually is the only option you have.

In the top right of the Settings pane, there is a pair of curly braces (visible in Figure 2-4). When you click them, the `settings.json` file for your current scope (user or workspace) is opened. Following is an example of what the file might look like:

```
{
    "workbench.colorTheme": "Default Light+",
    "workbench.sideBar.location": "left",
    "editor.lineNumbers": "off",
    "files.useExperimentalFileWatcher": true,
```

```
            "workbench.useExperimentalGridLayout": true,
            "terminal.integrated.shell.windows": "C:\\Program Files\\Git\\bin\\bash.exe",
            "editor.autoIndent": false,
            "diffEditor.renderSideBySide": true
    }
```

Each of the settings is a JSON attribute name combined with a value. The value can be a string, a Boolean, a number, or another JSON object. Because the settings are interpreted by either Visual Studio Code or an extension, it's up to the consumer to determine what the proper format is.

The attribute name is the fully qualified name of the settings. In general, the name is in the form of *target.setting*, where *target* is the component that will be using the setting and *setting* is the identifier for the setting.

The settings.json file is a text file, albeit one formatted as JSON. This means you are free to edit it as you wish. Make the changes you want, save the file, and the settings will be changed. If this seems a little free-form for you, know that IntelliSense is available to help ensure that you don't make any typos. Defining settings that aren't used by any extension does not cause Visual Studio Code to break. So long as the file is in a valid JSON format, Visual Studio Code has no problem.

This book is going to approach the Settings options a little differently than the other icons on the Activity Bar. As has already been mentioned, a large number of settings are available and simply listing them and describing their functionality doesn't provide the appropriate context to their usage (at least, not in a lot of cases). So instead, you'll find information about the settings that are appropriate alongside the corresponding functional description. If you need to find a summarized list of the settings that are covered by the book, you can find them in the index.

STATUS BAR

Like pretty much every other application you've worked with, the Status Bar in Visual Studio Code appears at the bottom of the application, and it runs across the entire width of the application's screen. What makes this Status Bar just a little bit different is that, along with providing status information, it can also be used to make adjustments to the settings for the current file, or to interact with source control.

There are two ends to the Status Bar, each with a different focus. The left side of the status bar, shown in Figure 2-6, is the status for the source control and the open project as a whole.

FIGURE 2-6

Four components are on the left side of the Status Bar. On the extreme left is the name of the current branch. In Figure 2-6, the project is on the *master* branch. The asterisk at the right of the branch name indicates that a change has been made to the current branch.

It's possible to initiate the process of changing branches from the Status Bar. Click the current branch and the text box and drop-down shown in Figure 2-7 appears at the top of the Visual Studio Code interface.

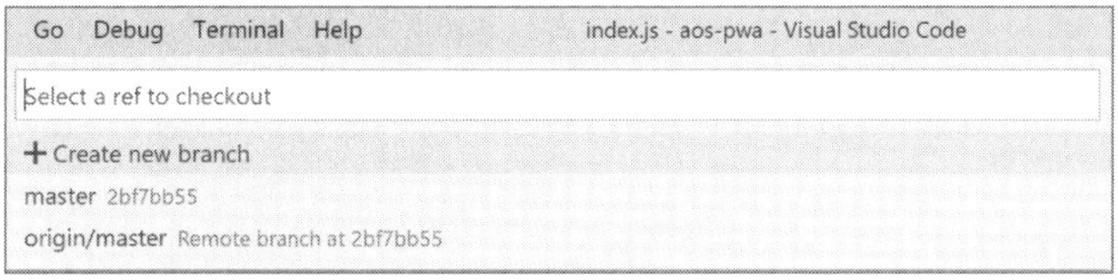

Go   Debug   Terminal   Help   index.js - aos-pwa - Visual Studio Code

Select a ref to checkout

\+ Create new branch

master 2bf7bb55

origin/master Remote branch at 2bf7bb55

FIGURE 2-7

Here you have a number of options. You can just select the branch to which you would like to change. Clicking a branch automatically performs the checkout. Or, you can start typing the name of the desired branch into the text box. This filters the list of branches that appear in the list. Again, selecting one initiates the checkout process.

Finally, you can create a new branch by clicking the Create New Branch link. A different text box is displayed, indicating that you should provide the name of the new branch. Type the name of the new branch and press Enter to create the branch. A branch with the same name is also created on the remote server. If you want to terminate the creation at any point, use the Esc key to exit this process.

The second icon (the circle of arrows in Figure 2-6) is used to synchronize changes with a Git repository. This icon actually changes to represent the action that is triggered when the icon is clicked. When it's the circle of arrows, it is used to synchronize changes between the current branch and the remote repository associated with the branch. As changes in the project are made, the icon will also change. There is a cloud/arrow icon that is used to publish changes to the local repository. You can find more details about the interactions with source control in Chapter 5.

The last two icons on the left side of the status bar (the ones at the right of that group) are used to indicate the errors and warnings that have been found within the project. The number of errors and warnings is indicated as a number to the right of the corresponding icons. When you click the icon (either one), the Problems window is displayed. The Problems window is described in its own section later in this chapter.

The group of icons on the right side of the Status Bar (shown in Figure 2-8) are focused on information and settings related to the current editor.

FIGURE 2-8

Starting from the left is the current position of the cursor, both the row and the column. If there is an active selection in the editor, the number of characters (even across rows) is displayed. If you click this information, a text box opens at the top of Visual Studio Code (see Figure 2-9) that allows you to enter a line number and go directly to that line. Ctrl+G opens the same text box.

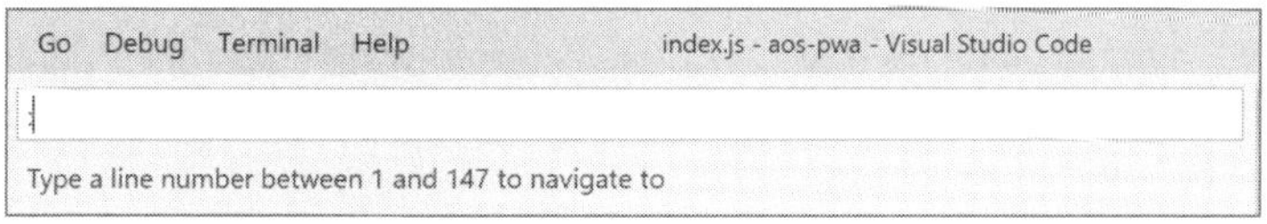

Go   Debug   Terminal   Help   index.js - aos-pwa - Visual Studio Code

Type a line number between 1 and 147 to navigate to

FIGURE 2-9

The next piece of information relates to code indentation within the editor. In Figure 2-8 each indentation consists of four spaces. However, you can change and configure this in a number of different ways. Clicking the value causes the panel shown in Figure 2-10 to appear at the top of the window.

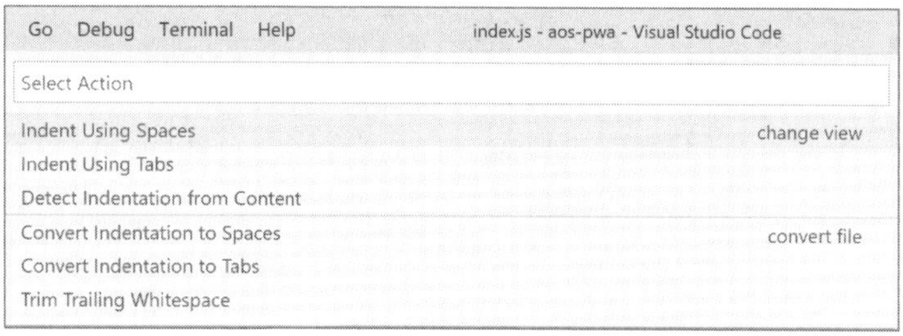

Go Debug Terminal Help	index.js - aos-pwa - Visual Studio Code
Select Action	
Indent Using Spaces	change view
Indent Using Tabs	
Detect Indentation from Content	
Convert Indentation to Spaces	convert file
Convert Indentation to Tabs	
Trim Trailing Whitespace	

FIGURE 2-10

In the top half of Figure 2-10, three options are available for indentation. Spaces can be used, which is the current setting for this file. Tabs can be used, by selecting that option. Or the characters used for indentation can be detected by examining the content. If your preference is to use spaces, clicking the Change View link at the right enables you to change the number of spaces.

Changing the number of spaces impacts the positioning of the indentation lines (the vertical lines seen in Figure 2-11). However, it does not change the positioning of code that had previously been created using a different indentation point.

FIGURE 2-11

The lower half of the pane is used to convert from space-based indentation to tab-based and back again. Clicking the top line (Convert Indentation To Spaces) will convert from tabs to spaces. Clicking the second line converts in the opposite direction, making each indentation tab the previously specified number of spaces. The bottom option has nothing to do with the indentation but will remove any extra spaces from the end of the lines in the file.

The next setting in this Status Bar group relates to the encoding for the current file. In Figure 2-8, the current setting is UTF-8. Clicking this item provides two options: you can save the file using a different encoding or you can reopen the file with a different encoding. Regardless of which choice you make, the next option is to select the desired encoding from a fairly long set of possibilities.

The next option (seen as CRLF in Figure 2-8) is the character sequence that appears at the end of each line. CRLF means that the line is terminated by a carriage return and a line feed. The other option, available if you click the setting, is to just have the line terminated by a line feed.

Next to the encoding option is the language being used in the current editor. By default, this is determined by using the extension on the file. However, by clicking this option, a pane appears (shown in Figure 2-12) that enables you to affect this value.

FIGURE 2-12

The bulk of the pane in Figure 2-12 is taken up with a list of the languages that are supported by Visual Studio Code. You can choose the language being used by simply selecting it.

A couple of other options are available to you, however. The first item, Auto Detect, will use the known information about the various languages in an attempt to determine what language is in the current editor.

The second choice, Configure File Association For .js, is used to modify the language that Visual Studio Code associates with this file extension. Choosing this option displays a list of languages, allowing you to select the one that will be chosen for future files with the same extension.

The next choice, the option labeled Configure 'JavaScript' Language Based Settings, is used to customize how the JavaScript language is processed within Visual Studio Code. Making this choice opens up the settings file for Visual Studio Code in a new editor. You can then manually add settings to this file and save them to have them take effect. The specific settings are dependent on the language involved.

The last two icons are used to get and send feedback about Visual Studio Code. The happy face icon opens up a window (shown in Figure 2-13) that can be used to tweet a message describing your thoughts.

Although sending a tweet is nice, the feedback pane also includes a couple of links to provide specific information to the development team. The Submit A Bug link triggers the form shown in Figure 2-14.

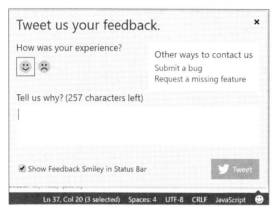

FIGURE 2-13

FIGURE 2-14

Here, you can choose the type of feedback (bug, feature request, or performance issue) and the target of the feedback (either Visual Studio Code itself or an extension). In addition, you will be asked for a title and a set of steps that will reproduce the bug or issue. Once the information has been provided, clicking Preview On GitHub causes this information to be transferred to GitHub.

Why GitHub, you ask? Because Visual Studio Code is an open-source project, and the source code is hosted on GitHub. So your feedback will, if you approve it, become an issue raised against that project.

The final icon at the extreme right of Figure 2-8 (the bell) is used to view any notifications that have been raised from within Visual Studio. These are not notifications associated with the project that you're working on, but more application-level notices, such as when a new version is available. Clicking the icon displays the list and enables you to view and respond to the notifications as appropriate.

OTHER WINDOWS

To this point, we've looked at the surface of Visual Studio Code as it's presented upon opening. This section discusses other windows that are quite useful and only a couple of keystrokes or clicks away.

Command Palette

One of the keys to be able to stay "in the flow" is to avoid removing your hands from the keyboard. To assist in getting to the various commands that are available in Visual Studio Code, you have the Command Palette at your disposal. Figure 2-15 shows the Command Palette at the top of the IDE.

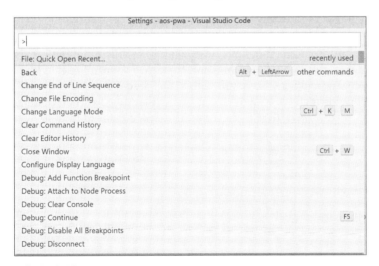

FIGURE 2-15

The Command Palette is activated through a number of different keystrokes. Keeping with the "in the flow" theme, you can launch it using Ctrl-Shift+P (Cmd+Shift+P in macOS) or F1. Those keyboard shortcuts are configurable in case you'd prefer a different combination. The "Keyboard Shortcuts" section in Chapter 4 describes the process of changing the shortcut. You can also open the palette through the View ⇨ Command Palette menu option.

The purpose of the palette is to give you access to all of the Visual Studio Code commands. As you can see from Figure 2-15, a list of all of the available commands is visible. For those commands that are associated with keyboard shortcuts, the corresponding shortcut appears to the right of the command.

As you type into the text box at the top, the list of commands is modified to indicate those that match that content. Through a setting (*Workbench: Keyboard Navigation*), you have the ability to control how the matching commands are revealed. This setting is actually used to control how text-based searches are revealed for all of the lists and trees in Visual Studio Code. Three options are available:

➤ *Simple*—As you type, the items in the list that match the accumulated keystrokes become focused. Matching is only done by the beginning of the item. In other words, the keystrokes 'work' would match 'workspace', but not 'network'.

➤ *Highlight*—As you type, the items in the list that match the accumulated keystrokes become highlighted. You can see the additional matching items by using the scroll bar to move up and down the list.

➤ *Filter*—As you type, all of the elements that don't match the accumulated keystrokes are filtered out of the list.

At the very top of the list are the commands that you have most recently used. The idea is that, over time, your favorite commands will remain within reach with a minimum number of keystrokes. You can control the number of recent commands that are kept through the *Workbench: Command-PaletteHistory* command. This value is just a number indicating how much history to persist. The history of commands spans executions of Visual Studio Code. If you would rather not keep any commands, set this value to 0.

Terminal Window

For many different project types, being able to execute commands from the command line is critical to functionality and productivity. A Terminal window is built into Visual Studio Code to help with this process (see Figure 2-16). You can launch the window using Ctrl+` (that's the backtick character), the View ⇨ Terminal menu option, or the *View: Toggle Integrated Terminal* command from the Command Palette.

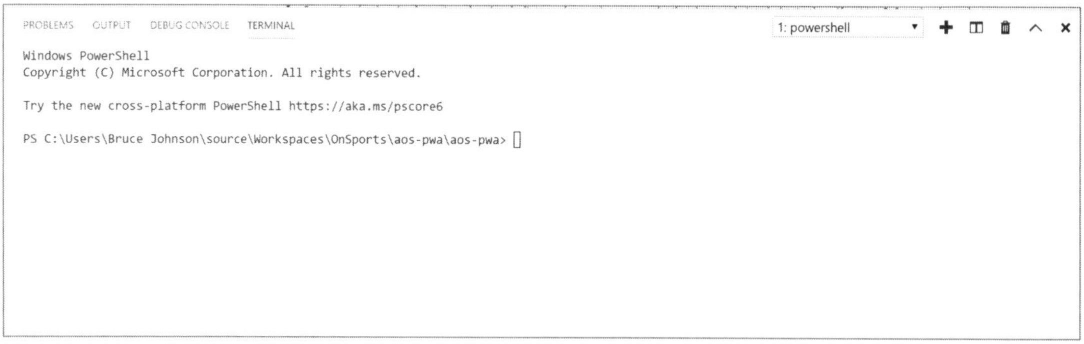

```
PROBLEMS   OUTPUT   DEBUG CONSOLE   TERMINAL                                    1: powershell        ▼  +  ⊞  🗑  ∧  ✕

Windows PowerShell
Copyright (C) Microsoft Corporation. All rights reserved.

Try the new cross-platform PowerShell https://aka.ms/pscore6

PS C:\Users\Bruce Johnson\source\Workspaces\OnSports\aos-pwa\aos-pwa> []
```

FIGURE 2-16

When the Terminal window is launched, the current directory is your current folder. The actual shell that is running depends on your platform. For macOS and Linux, the default is **$SHELL**. For Windows 10 it's PowerShell. For earlier versions of Windows, it's **cmd.exe**.

However, you can change the shell that gets launched at any time through the settings. Start by launching the Command Palette (Ctrl+Shift+P). Then enter **shell** into the text box. Select *Terminal: Select Default Shell* and a list of the shells for your platform appears (see Figure 2-17). Select the shell you want, and that shell becomes the one opened the next time you open a terminal.

FIGURE 2-17

It's possible to have more than one Terminal session running simultaneously. In Figure 2-16, toward the top right, there is a drop-down list. This list contains the different shells that you are currently running. Immediately to the right, there is a plus icon. Click that icon and you launch another shell (the shell that you have specified as the default). You can move from one shell to any of the others by using the drop-down.

If you want to look at two Terminal sessions side-by-side, click the two-panel icon to the right of the plus. This creates another Terminal session, but next to the current one (see Figure 2-18).

FIGURE 2-18

The garbage can icon is used to kill the current Terminal session. If you kill the last terminal session, the Terminal tab is closed.

A number of settings can be used to configure your Terminal window. For each of the different platforms, you can configure the path to the shell that will be executed (*Terminal ⇨ Integrated ⇨ Shell: Linux, Terminal ⇨ Integrated ⇨ Shell: Osx,* and *Terminal ⇨ Integrated ⇨ Shell: Windows*). You can specify parameters that are included when the shell is executed (*Terminal ⇨ Integrated ⇨ Shell Args: Linux/Osx/Windows*), and, in one of the most useful settings, you can specify the initial working directory for the shell (*Terminal ⇨ Integrated: Cwd*). This is particularly useful if the root directory for your folder is not convenient for the commands that you want to execute.

Output Window

Messages from various parts of Visual Studio Code are directed to the Output window (see Figure 2-19). You can get to this window using the View ⇨ Output menu option.

FIGURE 2-19

Functionally, the Output window is not particularly complex. Its job is to display output from the different processes that are running from within Visual Studio Code. In Figure 2-19, you can see a drop-down toward the top right of the window. This contains a list of all of the potential sources for output. To see the output for a source, select it in that drop-down. In Figure 2-19, the output is from Git.

To the right of that drop-down are a couple of useful icons. The first icon to the right (lines with an X in the top corner) is used to clear the Output window for the current source. This allows you to be able to focus on the output that is important to you.

The next icon (the lock) is very useful if the selected source generates frequent output. Whenever a source produces output, it is added to the bottom of the screen. When there is too much output, a scroll bar appears. All of this is pretty typical behavior. However, if you scroll back up through the output looking for something and the source generates another line, the text flicks back down to the bottom. This can be quite annoying if you're looking for that crucial message. When you click the lock icon, you freeze the window at your scroll point. This means that when a line gets added to the bottom, your current scroll point is not changed. The output remains stable and you can find that important message a lot easier.

The third icon (the document with the arrow) is not enabled for all sources. In fact, it's enabled only when one of the Log sources (at the bottom of the drop-down list in Figure 2-19) is selected. These logs are actually windows into the log files generated by different parts of Visual Studio Code. While they are visible in the Output Window, they are actually physical files on the file system. Clicking the icon causes the physical file to be opened in an editor.

Debug Console

The Debug Console (Figure 2-20) is quite similar in functionality to the Output window.

The difference between the two is that while the Output window is a view into different sources, the Debug Console only has a single source: the debugger.

The content of this window is generated while you are debugging your application. So all the messages generated by the debugger are sent to the Debug Console. As well, if your application directs messages to the debug output (by using the `console.log` method in JavaScript, for example), those messages also appear in the Debug Console.

FIGURE 2-20

In terms of control you have over the contents, there is an icon in the top right of the window (the lines with the X) that when clicked clears the contents of the window.

Problems Window

The Problems window (Figure 2-21) lists all the errors and warnings currently found in your project.

FIGURE 2-21

The display is in a hierarchical format. At the top of each tree is the file in which the errors or warnings are found. Then, below that node is a list of the errors and warnings, including the line and character position where they are. Double-clicking any of the items will open the editor for that file and position the cursor onto that line.

At the right side of the top bar in Figure 2-21 are a couple of other controls that can be useful when you have a lot of errors and warnings to sift through. First, there is a filter text box. Enter some text and only those errors and warnings that contain the text will appear in the window. There is also a gear button on the right side of the text box. This provides an automatic filter based on the *Files: Exclude* setting.

This setting controls which files appear in the Explorer tree. More specifically, it is a collection of *glob* patterns, which define the files and folders that are not to appear in the Explorer. The setting also is used to restrict which files or folders appear in the results when searching. For instance, you might not want to search through the files in the node_modules directory, because it contains third-party code. You can include a pattern in the Files: Exclude setting (see the example in the following section) and none of those files will be put into the search results.

GLOB PATTERNS

A glob pattern is a mechanism for specifying a set of files using wildcards. The name is a diminutive for *global* and comes from its usage in the Unix world going back to the 1970s. While the patterns look like regular expressions, the fact that they do not allow for multiple repetitions of the pattern means that they don't fit neatly into that category. Still, there is enough similarity for someone who knows regular expressions to recognize the patterns.

Building up a glob pattern is a matter of combining wildcards and literals to define a set of files. Table 2-1 describes the different types of wildcard matches that are available.

TABLE 2-1: Glob Pattern Wildcards

WILDCARD	DESCRIPTION
*	Matches zero or more of any character.
?	Matches any single character.
[abc]	Matches any one of the characters specified in the brackets. In this example, it would match either 'a', 'b', or 'c'.
[a–z]	Matches any one of the range of characters specified in the brackets.
[0–9]	Matches any one of the numeric characters specified in the brackets.
**	Matches zero or more path segments.

Here are a couple glob examples to give you an idea of some common patterns:

➤ `**/.git`—Matches the file named .git anyplace in the hierarchy for the current folders.

➤ `**/node_modules/*/**`—Matches all files underneath the node_modules directory found anyplace in the hierarchy for the current folders.

Also on the right of the Problems window shown in Figure 2-21, there is an icon (immediately to the right of the filter text box) that is used to collapse all of the errors and warnings so that only the list of files is visible.

A couple of other indicators within Visual Studio Code alert you when there are problems within your project. Figure 2-22 illustrates the Project view and Outline view when there are errors.

The screen on the left of Figure 2-22 is the Outline view. In this view, you can see that TabContainer has four errors and the require method has one. While it might not be obvious in the black and white image, the names TabContainer and require are in red, along with the number of errors.

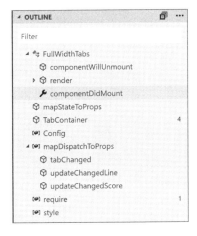

FIGURE 2-22

The screen on the right of Figure 2-22 is the Project view. At the bottom, you can see that index.js has six errors. The M indicates that the file has been modified but not saved. The index.js name is also in red. But, along with the name of the file, the names of its parent directories are also labeled in red. So both tabs and containers will be in red. This allows you to see where any errors are even if the tree has not been fully expanded.

SUMMARY

It should be apparent that the workspace is the focal point of the development experience. While most of your time might be spent in the editor, the workspace is the glue that holds all of the features together. In this chapter, you were introduced to the main features of the workspace and how those features can be customized. In the next couple of chapters, you will drill a little deeper into two areas that are critical to development success: the Explorer and the various editors.

3

Files and Folders and Projects (Oh My)

WHAT'S IN THIS CHAPTER?

➤ How to work with and navigate through the directory structure for your project

➤ Understanding the cross-platform components that make up Visual Studio Code

Your project has structure. Guaranteed. You might not always have complete control over the structure, but it's there, and you have to work with it.

In this chapter, we cover the visual components that Visual Studio Code has to help you navigate through your files and folders. This includes a detailed look at the Explorer, search functionality, and how you can tailor these to your liking.

EXPLORER

The purpose of the Explorer is to let you view and navigate through a tree view that contains the files and folders that make up your project. It looks similar to Figure 3-1.

To make the Explorer visible, you can click the Explorer icon in the Activity Bar (on the left of Figure 3-1), use the View ➪ Explorer menu option, or use a keyboard shortcut (defaulting to Ctrl+Shift+E or Cmd+Shift+E).

The Explorer consists of three sections. At the top is a list of open editors and editor groups. In the middle are the files and folders of your project. At the bottom, an outline of the currently active editor is displayed (assuming that the current editor supports the concept of an outline). The sections can be hidden or displayed by right-clicking at the top of the Explorer and checking (or unchecking) the context item related to the section. Because both the Open Editors and Outline sections of the Explorer deal with editing files, they are described in Chapter 4, "Editing Code in the Language of Your Choice."

FIGURE 3-1

Project View

The middle section of the Explorer (shown in Figure 3-2) contains a view of the files and folders that make up the current project. For the most part, the functionality found in the Project View mimics similar views in other editing tools. Folders are shown in a hierarchical manner. Clicking a folder opens it, displaying the files that are found inside. A second click on the folder closes the tree node, hiding all of the contained files.

To preview a file, click it. This opens the file in a tab within the currently active editor group. If you click a second file, it replaces the first file in the same tab. In other words, one tab is used to preview any file. That tab can be repositioned within the editor group, just like any other tab. If you've made a change to the first file, clicking a second file will create a different tab to be used to preview files.

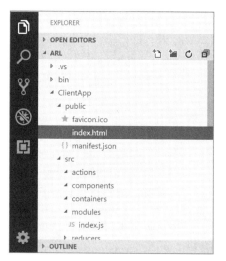

FIGURE 3-2

EDITOR GROUPS

Editor groups are covered in detail in Chapter 4, but it's worthwhile to briefly describe what they are. The large area to the right (by default) of the Explorer is where files are edited. That space is more accurately described as a container for one or more editor groups. An editor group is a collection of tabs and editors that can be positioned as a single unit. If you consider the editor group as the area where files are edited, that's a complete enough understanding for this chapter.

The Project View area also provides a number of both common and uncommon features for a file and folder view. First, the common features:

➤ You can drag files from your Explorer (that is, the file system explorer for your environment) into the Project View.

➤ You can select one or more files from the Project View and, using the context menu, copy or delete them.

➤ You can select a file from the Project View and, using the context menu, rename it.

➤ You can select one or more files from the Project View and drag them to another folder within the Project View. This effectively moves the files from one folder to another.

These are features that are to be expected from almost any file and folder view. Where Visual Studio Code starts to go beyond the common features starts with a couple of settings that can modify the flow of some of these features to make them more to your liking. The *Explorer: Enable Drag and Drop* setting determines whether you can move files or folders by dragging them. The *Explorer: Confirm Drag and Drop* setting determines whether you are prompted for a confirmation before moving the files or folders, and the *Explorer: Confirm Delete* setting is used to specify whether a deletion requires confirmation before deleting the selection.

You can select one or more files from the Project View and drag them onto an editor group. It will add editor tabs for those files in the group. If any of the files are already in the group, nothing happens to that tab.

From the context menu shown in Figure 3-3, you can choose from the following options.

Open to the Side—With one or more files selected, you can open them to the side. This will create a new editor group to the right of the currently active editor group and add the files to that new group.

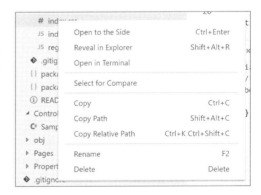

FIGURE 3-3

Reveal in Explorer—With one or more files selected, this option opens your local file system explorer to the directory in which the file(s) are found. If the selected files are in more than one directory, multiple instances of the explorer will open, one per directory.

Open In Terminal—With one or more files selected, this option launches the Terminal window with the initial directory set to the directory from the last selected file. The Terminal window is covered in detail in the "Terminal Window" section in Chapter 2, "Exploring the User Interface."

From the Explorer, it's possible to compare two files. The options that appear on the context menu are related directly to the number of files that you have selected. But to put the options into context, realize that the intent is to allow you to choose two files and compare them. The options are:

Select for Compare—This option is used to choose the first file in the comparison. If you have not selected a file for comparison previously and have only one file selected, it will be the only option available. Selecting this option chooses the selected file as the first file in the comparison. If there is already a first file, then this option replaces that file with the selected file.

Compare with Selected—This option is used to choose the second file in the comparison and to start the comparison. The option is available when you have one file selected and a first file in the comparison has already been chosen. It is also available when you have two files selected, in which case the comparison is performed on the selected files regardless of whether you had previously specified a file for comparison.

If you have more than two files selected, the context menu shows both the Select For Compare and Compare With Selected options. Choosing Compare With Selected will start the comparison between the file that had previously been selected for comparison and the first of the selected files. The Select For Compare option compares the last of the selected files to the file that had previously been selected.

That's a lot of different options and a lot of different ways that things work within these two context menu options. As was mentioned at the outset, keep in mind that the goal of the file comparison is to have you choose two files to compare. That viewpoint helps a great deal with answering any questions that arise.

The context menu has a number of other useful features. To add files and folders to your project, select an existing folder and right-click. At the top of the context menu are two options: New File and New Folder (see Figure 3-4). If you select a file, neither of these options will be available.

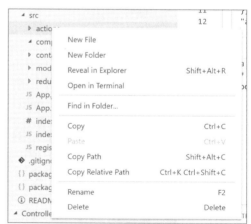

FIGURE 3-4

For those readers who might be familiar with adding new items in Visual Studio, the Visual Studio Code experience is quite different. Mostly, it just consists of entering a filename.

At the location where you selected the folder, a new item is added and a text box is visible where you can enter the name of the new item (see Figure 3-5). You just type the name of the new item, including the file extension.

FIGURE 3-5

The file extension is necessary because you don't specify the file type at any point in this process. There's no wizard that presents you with a list of possible file types and lets you select one. It's the file extension that is used to determine the file type and, of greater importance, the editor that will be used to edit the file. Because useful functionality like syntax coloring and IntelliSense are tied to the file editor, the file extension matters.

Along with impacting the editor for the file, the file extension also drives suggestions from Visual Studio Code. After you've added a new file, Visual Studio Code checks to see if you have installed any extensions to support the file type. If you haven't, Visual Studio Code checks the Marketplace for extensions that might be available. If one (or more) is found, a message indicating such appears at the bottom right of the interface (see Figure 3-6).

Naturally, you don't need to install the extension to be able to use the file. The most common file types already have editors that ship with Visual Studio Code. However, a lot of useful features are provided by the extensions, so it might be worth a look, especially for more esoteric file types. You'll find a more detailed look at how to use Extensions in Chapter 9, "Working with Extensions."

FIGURE 3-6

Along with the context menu, the Explorer also has a collection of icons at the right of the title area (see Figure 3-7). These icons are only visible when you mouse over the heading bar.

FIGURE 3-7

The four icons that are visible give quick access to four common functions. The two on the left are used to create a new folder and a new file, respectively. They are used if you are trying to create a file or folder at the top level of the folder you have open. The third icon (the arrowed circle) causes the Explorer to be refreshed based on the current files in the folder. The last button (at the right) is used to collapse all the nodes in the Explorer tree.

Speaking of the files and folders that appear in the Explorer, there is a setting that controls which ones are visible. The *Files: Exclude* setting is a collection of glob patterns. If a file matches one of the patterns, it is not visible in the Explorer. You can find a description of glob patterns in the "Problems Window" section in Chapter 2.

Decorations

Aside from evoking the impression of curtains, blinds, and knick-knacks, decorations in the Visual Studio Code Explorer provide a useful notification role. As you edit code, the files themselves enter different states—they could contain errors, they could have been changed since the last commit, or they might be untracked. Through decorations, Explorer can notify the developer of these conditions.

Figure 3-8 shows the Explorer with a number of different decorations visible on the right side. In general, the decorations come in two varieties. The circles are found at the folder level and indicate that, inside the folder, there is at least one file that is of interest. The color of the circle indicates the type of issue: pale red indicates an error, light gold means that files have been modified, and green is for files that are not currently being tracked by source control.

FIGURE 3-8

In Figure 3-8, the `.vscode` folder contains an untracked file. Both the `src` and `actions` folders contain a file with an error, and the `containers` folder contains modified files. Note that the `actions` folder also contains modified files, but the circle's color is pale red. That's because if there are multiple reasons for decorations in a folder, the color is provided by the most serious of the reasons.

Next to the `settings.json` file, there is a green "U". This indicates that the file is not currently being tracked by source control. Naturally, this decoration only appears if your workspace is currently associated with source control of some kind.

The `authenticate.js` file is a source for a couple of decorations. The numeric value (a "1" in this example) indicates the number of problems found in the file. This value (and the associated color) only appears if the offending file is open in one of the editors. The "M" at the end of the line means that the file has been modified and saved. You can see that a number of other files in the `actions` folder have also been modified, but have no errors in them. If you want to see a description of the reason for the decoration, hover over the file or folder and a tooltip appears (Figure 3-9).

FIGURE 3-9

Workspaces

Although it hasn't been talked about much to this point, when you are operating within the Explorer, you are working in a workspace. This is the name given to the collection of files and folders that are being worked on. It's not necessary that you are even aware of workspaces—for many developers, just opening a file or a folder and making changes is all there is to it. However, there are benefits to using workspaces, especially if you're working with multiple folders simultaneously.

Saving the Workspace

Although every opened folder is part of a workspace, none of the benefits start accruing until you save the workspace. To save the workspace, choose the File ⇨ Save Workspace As menu option. In the dialog that appears, you determine where you want to save a file with an extension of .code-workspace .

The .code-workspace file is not a project file or a solution file—it's just another configuration file. The schema for the configuration file is pretty straightforward, as shown in the following code snippet:

```
{
    "folders": [
        {
            "name": "PWA",
            "path": "aos-pwa"
        },
        {
            "name": "API",
            "path": "AosPwa.WebAPI"
        }
    ],
    "settings": {
        "workbench.quickOpen.closeOnFocusLost": false
    }
}
```

At the top level, there are two attributes in the example. The first, named folders, is an array of the folders in the workspace. The path attribute defines the path to the folder to be opened. The path is relative to the location of the .code-workspace file.

The name attribute provides a different title that gets displayed. Figure 3-10 illustrates what the Explorer looks like with the name attribute set.

As you can see, the name (PWA or API) appears at the top of each folder. If you don't include a name attribute, the name of the folder is used. That name attribute is really there to provide a more user-friendly version of the folder name. As well, the name given to the .code-workspace file is the name of the workspace and it appears at the top of the files and folders tree. In Figure 3-10, the name of the workspace is "AOS-MOBILE."

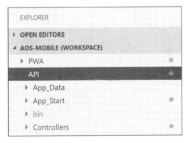

FIGURE 3-10

Adding Folders

You can add folders to a workspace even before you have saved the workspace. You do this through the File ➪ Add Folder To Workspace menu option. The standard Open File dialog appears, and you choose a folder to add.

Also, Visual Studio Code supports adding a folder by dragging it from your local file explorer and dropping it into the Explorer area. You can add multiple folders by selecting multiple folders from the Open File dialog, or by dragging multiple folders into the Explorer.

If you have not yet saved your workspace, the name of the workspace is "UNTITLED WORK-SPACE." This will change as soon as you save the workspace under a different name.

Settings

You might have noticed that the workspace configuration file also includes a `settings` attribute. Those are the workspace-level settings. But it's also possible to define settings that apply not just to the user and workspace, but also to the individual folders. The Settings editor includes this capability. Figure 3-11 illustrates the user interface for the AOS-MOBILE workspace.

FIGURE 3-11

To access the folder-level settings, select the folder from the drop-down list and edit the settings as usual.

One of the considerations from folder-level settings is how to handle collisions. That is, how does Visual Studio Code deal with the same setting being given different values by a user, workspace, or folder? For many settings, it's not a problem. The folder takes precedence. However, there are cases where this isn't possible. In particular, if there are settings that impact the entire development environment (such as the editor layout or zoom level), the folder-level setting is ignored. Settings that are ignored are grayed out when you are editing from within Visual Studio Code.

SEARCH

The file and folder search functionality in Visual Studio Code is available through a pane that, by default, replaces the Explorer in the interface. You launch search using a couple of different mechanisms. You can click the Search icon in the Activity Bar, you can use the Ctrl+Shift+F keyboard shortcut, or you can use the View ➪ Search menu option. The basic search interface is shown in Figure 3-12.

FIGURE 3-12

The functionality is relatively straightforward: type the term you want to search for into the text box and hit Enter. The list that appears below the text box (shown in Figure 3-13) shows the results.

The results are structured as a tree. Each file that contains at least one match appears as a node. The name of the file appears, along with the containing folder, relative to the top folder in your project. To the far right of the node, a number indicates the number of times the search term was found in the file. If you want to remove a file from the results, hover your mouse over the node and the number of results is replaced with an X. Clicking that X dismisses the results found in that file from the display.

The children for each file are the lines within the file where the search term is found. The tooltip for the line (visible on a mouse hover) is the entire line of code—actually, just the first 80 characters or so, but enough so that you can tell the details of the line.

FIGURE 3-13

Each line can be used to open the corresponding file in the editor and position the cursor on that line. A setting called *Workbench ➪ List: Open Mode* controls what you need to do to accomplish this. Two options are available. With Single Click, which is the default value, all that is required to open the file is to click it once. The other choice, Double Click, means that a double-click is required to open the file. This setting controls not only how the action on the Search results lines works, but also how actions on any tree or list work.

Advanced Searches

The functionality of the Search pane is not unlike many other searches. But Visual Studio Code also includes some advanced features, which are quite handy as you're trying to reduce the number of lines returned, or if you're just looking for a different combination of terms.

On the right side of the Search text box are three icons. The icon on the left is used to control whether the search is performed in a case-sensitive or case-insensitive manner. The default is case insensitive. When case sensitivity is selected, the icon is outlined by a box. Clicking the icon toggles the sensitivity on and off.

The second icon is used to toggle whole word matching. When selected (the icon is outlined in a box), only instances where the search term is an entire word are included. The default is not to use whole words, and clicking the icon toggles the setting.

The third icon toggles on and off the regular expression pattern-matching functionality. The details are described in the next section.

Regular Expression Matching

You can do more than just match the term you enter into the Search text box. You can provide a regular expression that is then processed against each line in each file. To turn this functionality on, click the icon to the extreme right of the Search text box. At this point, the entered term must be a valid regular expression in order for the search to function. Consider the examples in Table 3-1 of how regular expressions can be a powerful addition to your toolset.

TABLE 3-1: Regular Expression Examples

EXPRESSION	RESULT
Status ?Code	Matches either "Status Code" or "StatusCode," as the space is marked as an option character.
Stat.*Code	The ".*" combination matches one or more characters, so this covers StatCode and StatusCode.
[sS]tatusCode	Matches both the Pascal and Camel case versions of StatusCode.

You have available to you the full range of regular expression control characters. Though it can be difficult to learn, the ability to utilize regular expressions makes searching even more powerful.

Specifying Files

By default, all of the files in your project are included in the search. To be a little more precise, there are two settings that control the files that are searched. The *Files: Exclude* setting (described in the "Project View" section earlier in this chapter) controls the files that appear in your project by identifying (using a collection of glob patterns) the files and folders that are excluded. As you might expect, these files are not included in the search.

However, there is also a setting called *Search: Exclude* that defines (also through a collection of glob patterns) the set of files that, while they are part of the project, you do not want to be part of any search results. An example of the kinds of files you'd like to exclude from your search would be the `node_modules` directory or the `bower_components` directory. These would be third-party components that are part of your project but are not really something you are likely to want to search.

Both of those settings are part of the default functionality of the Search pane. But you can modify the files being searched without modifying the settings. If you click the ellipsis immediately below the Regular Expression toggle icon, a couple of additional text boxes become visible, as shown in Figure 3-14.

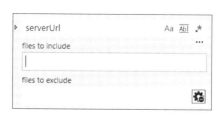

The top text box is used to specify the files that you'd like to include in your search results. For instance, if you enter the word **reduce**, only files or folders that contain the text "reduce" appear in the search results.

FIGURE 3-14

Aside from entering text, some special characters can be used to perform pattern matching. Table 3-2 contains these characters and their purpose.

TABLE 3-2: File Include Patterns

PATTERN	DESCRIPTION
*	Matches one or more characters in the filename or path.
?	Matches a single character in the filename or path.
**	Matches any number of path segments in folder path
{}	Contains a comma-separated list of patterns to match.
[]	Defines a range of alphanumeric characters to match.

The second text box is used to define the files and folders to be excluded from the search. The same rules as defined for the Files To Include text box apply. The difference is what Visual Studio Code does with the information. Here, files and folders that match the pattern are not included in the search results, even though they might normally be based on the Search settings. The gear icon at the right of the text box is used to toggle the exclusion pattern matching on and off.

Replacing Text

It's possible to replace text through the Search pane. To start the process, click the triangle to the left of the Search text box to reveal a second text box (see Figure 3-15).

FIGURE 3-15

In the second text box, enter the text that you'd like to replace the text in the first text box with. As you type, you can see the replacement take place in the search results. Figure 3-16 illustrates what this would look like.

Hitting Enter at this point performs the replacement on the first instance. Clicking the icon to the right of the second text box performs the replacement on all of the instances throughout all of the files in the search result.

FIGURE 3-16

Settings

A number of additional settings impact where and how the results can be viewed, as well as the results that actually appear:

➤ *Editor ⇨ Find: Seed Search String from Selection*—When this setting is checked, any text that has been selected in the editor automatically appears in the Search pane.

➤ *Search: Collapse Results*—Determines whether the search results will be expanded or collapsed. The default setting is auto, which means that files containing less than 10 results are expanded, and files that contain 10 or more results are collapsed. The other settings, AlwaysExpand and AlwaysCollapse, have the results expanded or collapsed, respectively, regardless of the number of results in a file.

➤ *Search: Maintain File Search Cache*—Visual Studio Code improves its search performance by using a search service process. This process indexes the contents of the file, as well as keeping track of any changes, so that when you perform a search, the results are very quickly generated. After an hour of non-use, the service is shut down. If this setting is checked, the search service process will continue running even if there is no activity.

➤ *Search: Show Line Numbers*—When checked, the line number within the file where the result is found is displayed.

➤ *Search: Smart Case*—If the pattern is all lowercase, the search will be performed in a case-insensitive manner. If there are any capital letters in the pattern, the search is case sensitive.

➤ *Search: Use Ignore Files*—The Files: Exclude setting is used to identify the files that will not be included in any search result. However there are a couple of files, `.gitignore` and `.ignore`, that are regularly used to specify files that are, well, ignored by different processes. This setting determines if the Search will also ignore those files.

SUMMARY

The folders and files that make up your project are an important part of the development process. In this chapter, you saw how you can use the Explorer and Search panes in Visual Studio Code to your advantage as you navigate through your application. Using the tools that are available to you can help improve your flow. Finding code, replacing text, and easily recognizing the changes you made are important parts of that flow.

Editing Code in Your Language of Choice

WHAT'S IN THIS CHAPTER?

➤ Learning the basic functionality provided by the editor and editor groups

➤ Understanding the advanced features that Visual Studio Code provides

➤ Customizing the editor to fit your personal coding style

Visual Studio Code is an editor. While many, many features and extensions are available, at its core, the editing functionality is of paramount importance. In this chapter, we look at the many ways there are to edit a file, the functions and shortcuts that are available to make your life easier, and how you can configure the editor to be what you need it to be.

EDITOR AREA

Figure 4-1 is a repeat of the overall view of Visual Studio Code that appeared in Figure 2-1. The Editor area is on the right side, labeled B. This is the space where editors for all of the files you have opened will appear.

By default, the top of the Editor space is a set of tabs, one tab per open file (see Figure 4-2).

Each tab contains an icon associated with the file type (for example, JS for JavaScript, C# for C# files, and a hash character [#] for CSS files). The name of the file appears in the middle. To get the full path for the file, hover over the tab with the mouse and the path appears as a tooltip. On right of the active tab is either an X or a filled-in circle. Clicking the X closes the tab. The circle indicates that the file has been modified, but not yet saved. Once the file is saved, the right icon goes back to an X. For currently inactive tabs, the X that is used to close the tab appears when the mouse hovers over the tab.

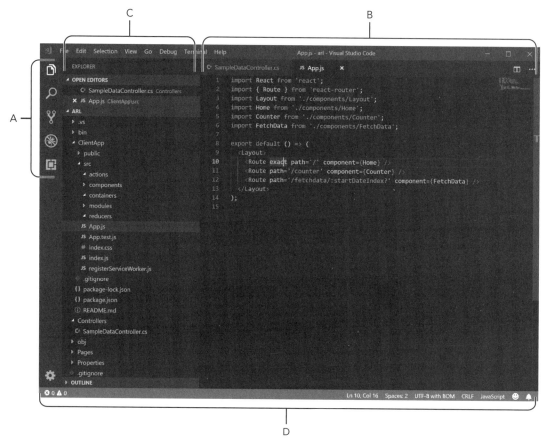

FIGURE 4-1

FIGURE 4-2

But if you're like many developers, the area along the top of the Editor space isn't enough. When that happens, some of the tabs will be removed from the top. You can access a list of the currently open files by clicking the More button (the ellipsis at the right of the toolbar shown in Figure 4-3) and choosing the Show Opened Editors menu option.

FIGURE 4-3

You'll notice that the text box at the top of the list of opened editors has the characters *edt* in it. This area is known as the *Command Palette* and it is very useful to help navigate through the large number of commands found in Visual Studio Code. But in this instance, the `edt` command is used to show a list of all the opened editors. You can make an editor active by clicking the item in the list.

Editor Groups and Layouts

As described in Chapter 3, "Files and Folders and Projects (Oh My)," the Editor space under discussion is more accurately called an editor group. This group holds a collection of tabs and editors and can be positioned as a single unit. You can create an editor group in three ways.

At the right of the tables (to the left of the More button) is an icon that adds an editor group to the right of the current group (see Figure 4-4).

FIGURE 4-4

The result from adding an editor group to the right of the group shown in Figure 4-2 is shown in Figure 4-5.

In the left group, all of the tabs that were there originally are still there. In the right group, the tab that was active is visible.

FIGURE 4-5

The second way to create an editor group is to right-click one of the tabs. This opens a context menu (shown in Figure 4-6) that includes the following four options:

➤ *Split Up*—Creates a new group above the current group

➤ *Split Down*—Creates a new group below the current group

➤ *Split Right*—Creates a new group to the right of the current group

➤ *Split Left*—Creates a new group to the left of the current group

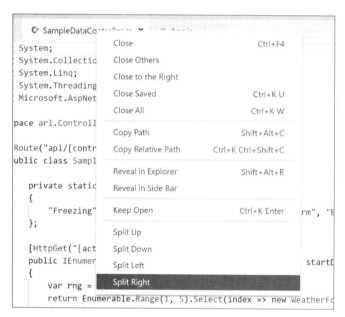

FIGURE 4-6

Figure 4-7 illustrates what happens when a Split Down has been performed.

The third way to create editor groups is through the View menu. Select the View ⇨ Editor Layout option to get to the menu shown in Figure 4-8.

At the top, you can see the same four options that were available in the context menu from Figure 4-6. At the bottom, there is also a Flip Layout option that will take groups that are side-by-side and transform them to groups that are one above the other.

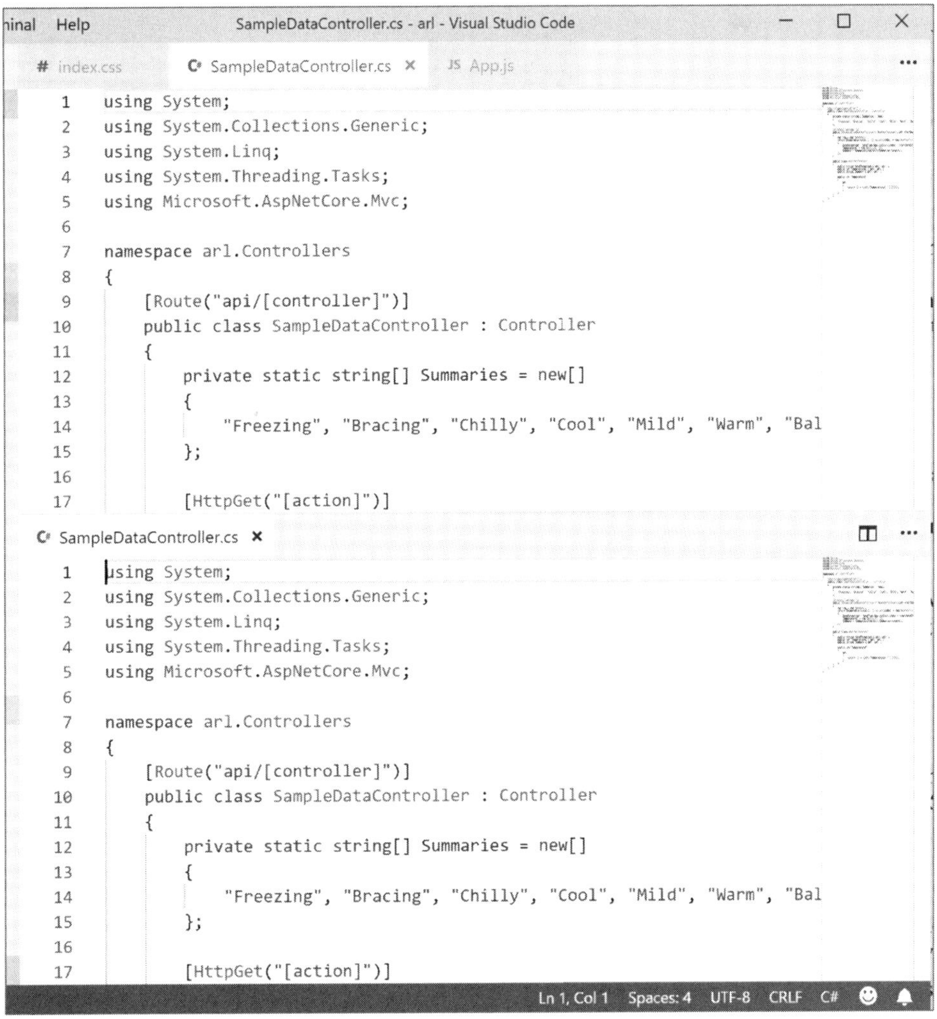

FIGURE 4-7

These various menu options are not the only ways to position files or groups within the Editor workspace. While the menus allow for vertical or horizontal columns, you can drag and drop files and groups to different locations.

Figure 4-9 illustrates the dragging of one file down to the bottom or the right vertical column. The shaded area is the section into which the new group is placed. The result is shown in Figure 4-10.

FIGURE 4-8

Other options are available if you prefer to work with some predefined editor group layouts. In Figure 4-8 there were a number of layouts from which to choose.

➤ Two Columns and Three Columns—Creates a total of two or three vertical groups.

➤ Two Rows and Three Rows—Creates two or three horizontal groups.

➤ Grid—Creates four editor groups, two on each row.

➤ Two Rows Right—Creates three editor groups in total, where the two on the right are stacked. Figure 4-10 shows a Two Rows Right layout.

➤ Two Columns Bottom—Also creates three groups, with the two on the bottom arranged side-by-side.

Open Editors

The Explorer was described in its own section in Chapter 3. There were three separate parts to the Explorer, and the center one (the project structure) was covered in detail in that chapter. Here, we look at the other two parts, the Open Editors and the Outline View. Figure 4-11 is an example of the Explorer.

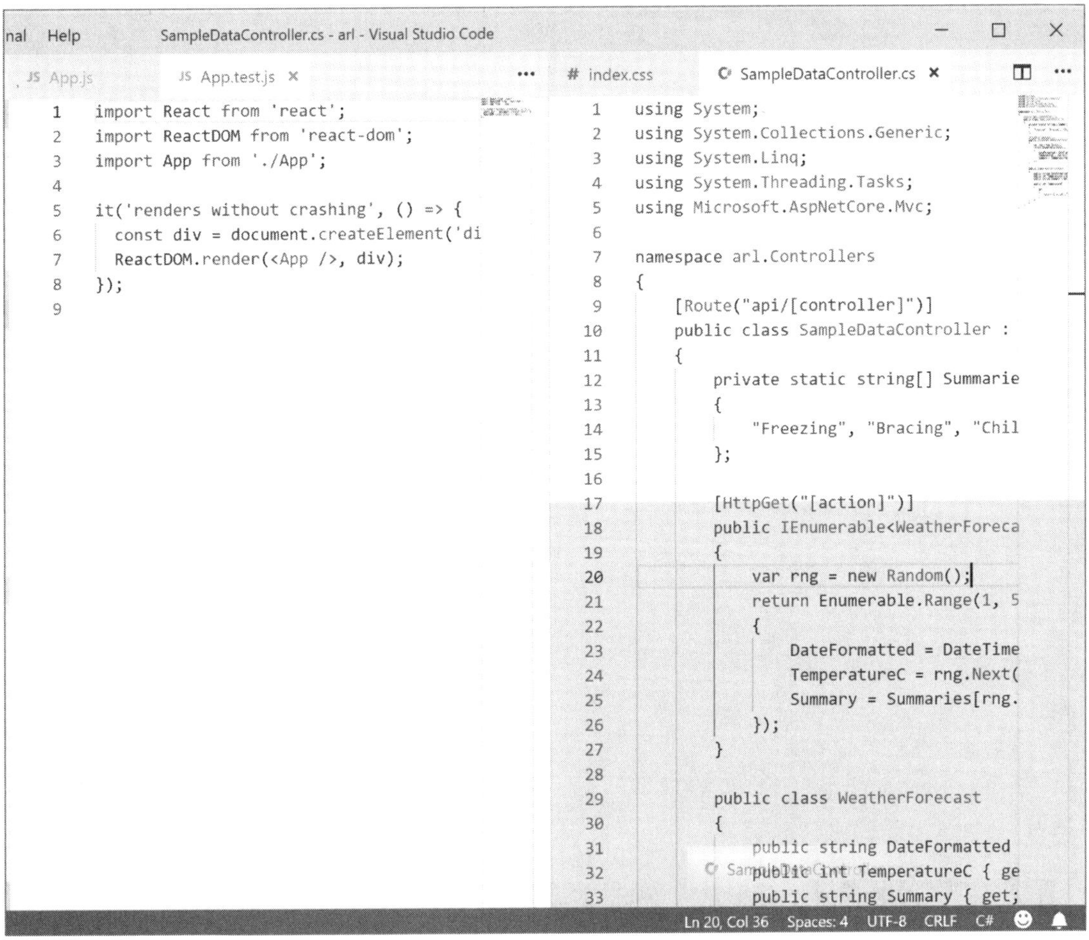

FIGURE 4-9

At the top of the Explorer (and collapsed in Figure 4-11) is the Open Editors section. Shown expanded in Figure 4-12, this section shows the editor groups and the files contained in each in a tree format.

The groups are numbered (Group 1, Group 2, Group 3, and so on) and the files in each appear below the group name. You can change the currently active file for a particular group by clicking it, and you can close a file by clicking the X that appears to the left of the filename. The X appears either when the file is active or if the mouse hovers over the filename.

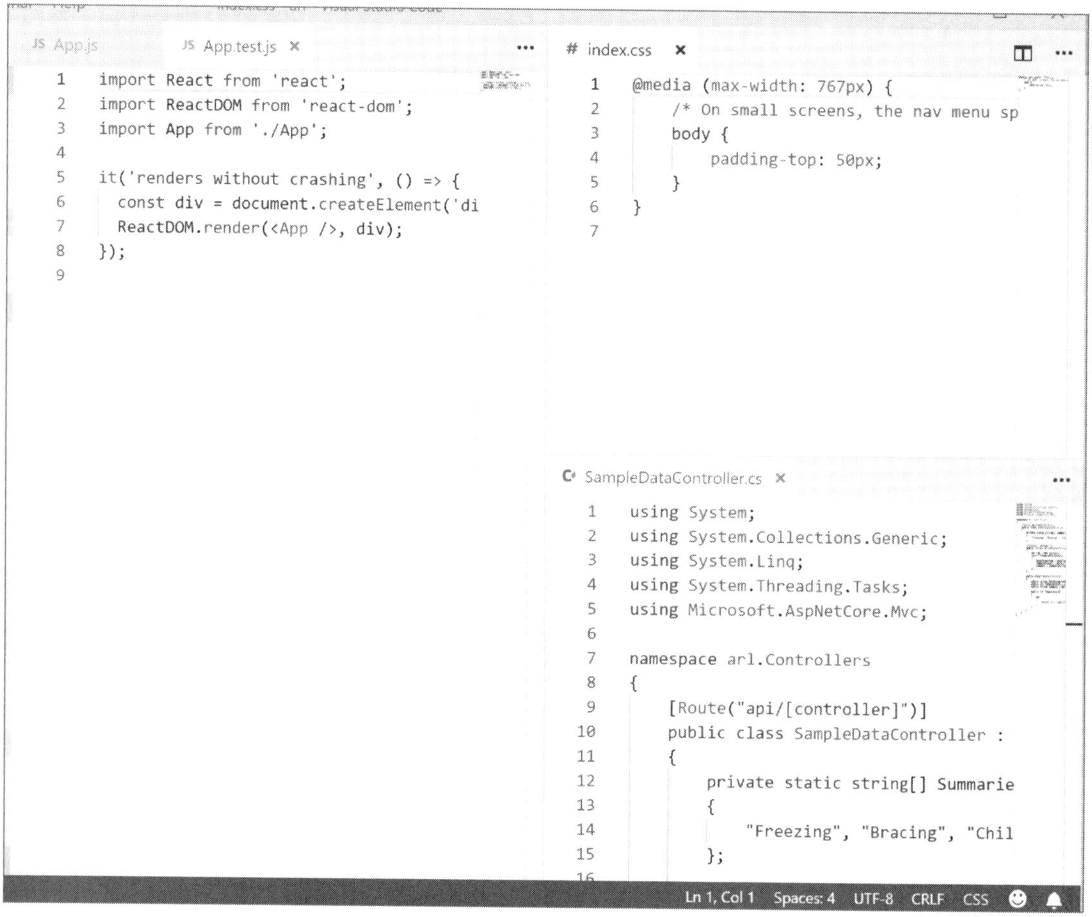

FIGURE 4-10

It's also possible to perform a number of collective actions, either on an individual group or on all of the open items. To the right of the label (visible in Figure 4-12) are up to three icons that only become visible on a mouse hover. The Open Editor icons (all three) are visible when the mouse is over any part of the Open Editor section. The group-level icons are only visible when the mouse is over a group.

The Open Editor icons show three options. The leftmost icon is used to toggle between a horizontal and vertical layout of the groups. The middle icon saves all of the currently unsaved files across all of the editor groups. The right icon closes all of the files, again across all of the editor groups.

For the group-level icons, the left icon saves all the unsaved files in that group, while the right icon closes all of the editors in that group.

FIGURE 4-11

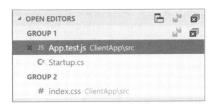

FIGURE 4-12

Outline View

The Outline View section of the Explorer is going to be either a useful section or one that can easily be ignored, depending on the types of files you work with most frequently. The purpose of the Outline View is to work with the editor for the current file to display the contents of that file as a hierarchical outline. Probably the easiest way to visualize the Outline View is with a couple of examples. In Figure 4-13, you can see the Outline View for a `package.json` file.

FIGURE 4-13

Each of the properties in the `package.json` file maps to a node in the outline tree. The text in the node is the property name. If the property is an object, the icon to the left of the name shows a pair of matching curly braces and the node becomes the parent for the properties within the object.

For the properties that are not objects, the icon to the left of the property name indicates the data type. At the bottom of Figure 4-13, the *abc* icon (next to the `name` and `version` properties) indicates a text property and the double-arrow icon (next to the `private` property) indicates a Boolean. If the property value is numeric, the icon is a number sign (hash symbol).

For a different example, see Figure 4-14. This is the outline view for a JavaScript file, specifically a React component.

The tree structure seen with the JSON file is still present. The difference is what makes up the nodes and the icons that are visible. At the top is the component itself, called `Full-WidthTabs`. The nodes with the cube at the left are methods found within the `FullWidthTabs` component.

You'll notice that methods are not necessarily the leaf of the tree. Within the `render` method, there are a number of children, such as `classes` and `currentTab`. These are variables defined within the `render` method. Yes, that icon that looks like a blob inside square brackets somehow means "variable."

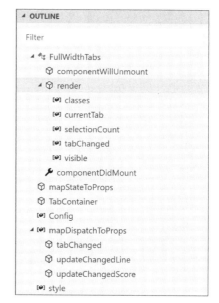

FIGURE 4-14

The other unusual notation is in the `mapDispatchToProps` variable, which would appear to contain methods based on the icons. That's because `mapDispatchToProps` is a function variable that returns a JSON object that has three functions as properties. So yes, it does make sense within the capabilities of JavaScript.

Part of the point is that the Outline View is very specific to the editor that is currently active. Not all editors support the Outline View, and the icons and content are going to vary for each one. It's not nearly within the scope of the book to cover all of the different outline views—not to mention that they could easily be changed or added to with updates to Visual Studio Code. Suffice it to say that hovering over any of the nodes will provide a slightly more detailed description of the content, information that will provide the necessary context for the editor.

EDITING FUNCTIONALITY

As was mentioned at the outset of the chapter, Visual Studio Code is an editor (a text editor, really). As a text editor, it has a lot of features that are aimed at making your life easier as you work with your code. In this section, we take a detailed look at the many different features that you can bring to bear on your tasks.

Keyboard Shortcuts

One of the keys to productive editing is the ability to keep your hands on your keyboard as much as possible. Although using the mouse is sometimes necessary, being able to perform some of the most common editing functions, like moving the cursor, selecting blocks of text, and adding code snippets, using only keyboard chords is pretty powerful.

If you're not familiar with the term, by the way, a *keyboard chord* is a combination of keys that are depressed simultaneously in order to perform a function. Things like Ctrl+X and Ctrl+C (cut and copy, respectively) are commonly used keyboard chords. But any two- or three- character combinations are referred to as a chord.

A collection of default keyboard shortcuts is available for each platform, and the chords used to trigger the shortcut are different on each platform. So a big list of the chords and the functionality in each would be voluminous and not particularly enlightening.

Instead, this book is going to treat the shortcuts a little like it treats the settings. This starts with a discussion of some of the most common editing shortcuts that are supported. For shortcuts that are not part of the editor, mention will be made in the appropriate chapter. Next, the process of customizing the shortcuts is described. As part of the customization process, you can actually see the keyboard chord used to trigger the shortcuts for your specific platform.

With that in mind, what follows is a list of some frequently useful keyboard shortcuts that relate to editing code. The command name is what is maintained in common across the platforms:

➤ *Add Line Comment, Remove Line Comment*—Adds or removes the comment character at the beginning of the current line. If more than one line is selected, the comment character is added to the beginning of each line.

➤ *Add Selection to Next Find Match*—Starts to perform a Find Next match using the selected text. The matches are highlighted in the editor and successive executions of this command move from one match to the next throughout the file.

➤ *Auto Fix*—Used when you have an issue with your code and potential solutions have been identified through IntelliSense. For a given issue, IntelliSense might include one or more possible fixes. This command causes the first fix in that list (typically, the most likely one) to be implemented.

➤ *Change All Occurrences*—Takes the current selection and finds all occurrences in the current file. The cursor is positioned at the end of each of these selections. Figure 4-15 illustrates what this looks like.

As you start typing, the changes made are applied to all of the selected occurrences simultaneously. In the editor, the dark, horizontal bars on the left of the editing area indicate where in the file occurrences have been found.

```
JS authenticate.js  ✕

              UPDATE_USER_NAME_FAIL,
              SET_USERID_TO_CURRENT,
              LOGOUT,
              PASSWORD_RESET,
              PASSWORD_RESET_FAIL,
        } from '../reducers/authenticate';
 20
        var Config = require('Config');

        export function validateUser(userId, password) {
            return function (dispatch)  {
                return new Promise((resolve, reject) => {
                    fetch(Config.serverUrl + '/api/account/jsonlogin',
                    {
```

FIGURE 4-15

➤ *Close Window*—Closes the current window. You are prompted to confirm whether you want changes to be saved or discarded upon closing.

➤ *Copy/Cut/Paste*—These are three standard commands that are available in every editor.

➤ *Copy Line Up/Copy Line Down*—Replicates the current line (the one that has the cursor) either above or below the current line. If multiple lines are selected, these commands aren't available.

➤ *Delete Line*—Deletes the current line. If multiple lines are selected, all the selected lines are deleted.

➤ *Expand Selection*—This command does what the name suggests: it expands the current selection by adding to it. The interesting part of the command is how the addition is determined. Starting from nothing being selected, expanding the selection adds, in the following order, current word, current code line, current line (including all leading and trailing whitespace), current block. An example helps to understand this.

Figure 4-16 shows four images. The top one illustrates the selection when the Expand Selection command is executed while the cursor is in "Promise." The second image shows after a second Expand Selection has been executed. Now the code for the entire line has been selected. The third image is after another command and the entire line is selected. The bottom image is after one more Expand Selection command and now the block that contains the original cursor is selected. Subsequent executions of the command will now select the parent blocks until, eventually, the entire code file is selected.

➤ *Find*—Initiates the Find process within the file. You can find details about the Find functionality in the "Find and Replace" section later in this chapter.

➤ *Find Next, Find Previous*—Used to move to the next or previous match. The most interesting part of these commands is that if the Find pane isn't already open, the command causes the pane to be opened, the currently selected value is displayed, and that text becomes the match to which the cursor is moved.

➤ *Fold All, Fold All Block Comments, Fold All Regions*—While folding might not be familiar to you as a term, the functionality quite likely is. Figure 4-17 illustrates code folding in a JavaScript file.

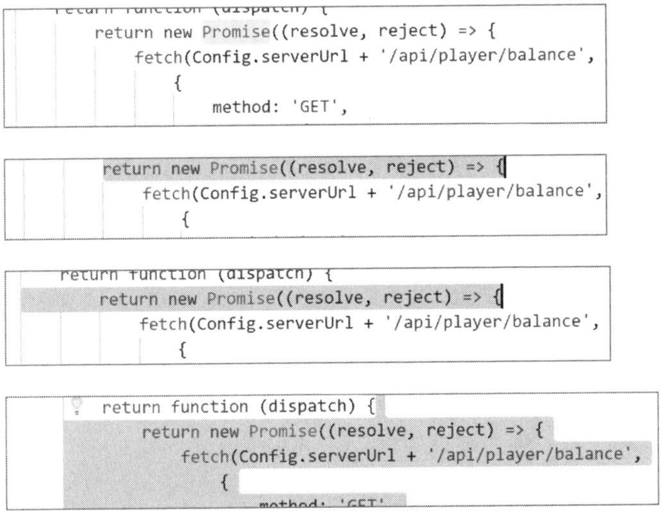

```
      return function (dispatch) {
        return new Promise((resolve, reject) => {
          fetch(Config.serverUrl + '/api/player/balance',
            {
              method: 'GET',
```

```
        return new Promise((resolve, reject) => {
          fetch(Config.serverUrl + '/api/player/balance',
            {
```

```
      return function (dispatch) {
        return new Promise((resolve, reject) => {
          fetch(Config.serverUrl + '/api/player/balance',
            {
```

```
    return function (dispatch) {
      return new Promise((resolve, reject) => {
        fetch(Config.serverUrl + '/api/player/balance',
          {
            method: 'GET'
```

FIGURE 4-16

```
render() {
    const { classe
    const { propsD

    return (
        <div clas
            <Grid
            <Lis
```

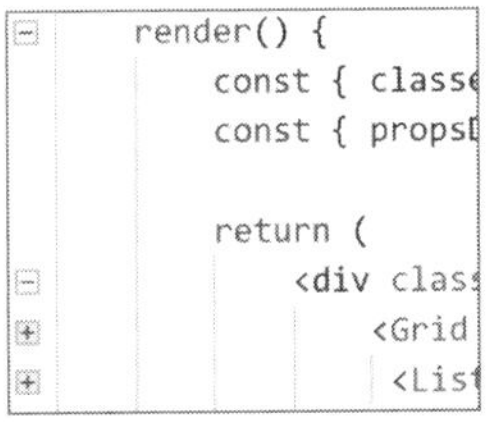

FIGURE 4-17

You'll notice the collection of plus and minus symbols to the left of the lines of code. Clicking a minus causes the code within that element to collapse. Clicking a plus causes the code within the section to expand. This is *code folding*.

A number of commands are related to code folding. They are:

➤ *Fold All*—Collapses all the code regions within the current file so that they are closed. Figure 4-18 illustrates a completely folded file.

➤ *Fold All Block Comments*—Collapses all block comment sections. The characters used to create a block comment depends on the language, but conceptually, it's a comment section that is delimited at both the start and end. This distinguishes it from a line comment, where the comment characters are at the beginning of each line.

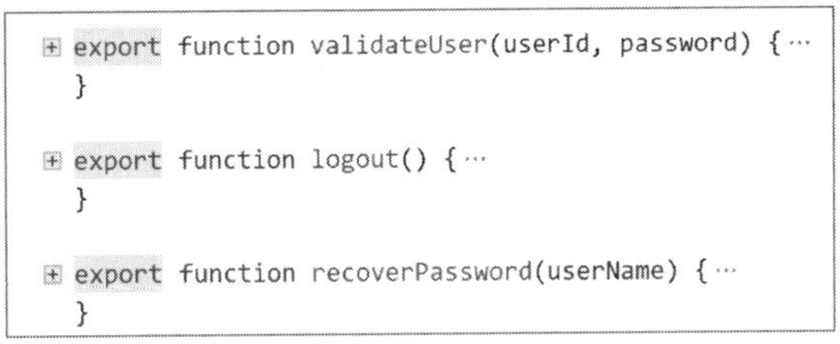

```
export function validateUser(userId, password) { ...
}

export function logout() { ...
}

export function recoverPassword(userName) { ...
}
```

FIGURE 4-18

➤ *Fold All Regions*—Some languages allow for the specific definitions of regions within the code file. This is opposed to regions being automatically determined based on, for example, the indentation level or scope blocks within the code. This command collapses all the explicitly defined regions.

➤ *Fold Level n*—There are a number of folding level comments. These commands will perform folding at the level specified by *n*. For instance, the Fold Level 2 command will collapse all of the second-level blocks.

➤ *Fold Recursively*—Starting at the level of folding for the current cursor position, folds the current block and all its child blocks.

➤ *Unfold*—Expands the current region, based on the cursor position.

➤ *Unfold All*—Expands all of the code regions in the current file.

➤ *Unfold All Regions*—If the current editor allows for the definition of a region, this command will expand all of those regions.

➤ *Unfold Recursively*—Starting at the level of folding for the current cursor position, this command unfolds the current block and all its child blocks.

Visual Studio Code includes some settings that impact the folding commands:

➤ Editor: Folding—Controls whether code folding is turned on or off.

➤ Editor: Folding Strategy—Determines how Visual Studio Code identifies the elements that can be folded. The default strategy of "auto" allows the language editor to determine the strategy. This is usually the preferred choice because the language understands the context of the code more intimately and is therefore better positioned to determine which elements can be collapsed. If you set the strategy to be "indentation," it uses the indentation level to determine the foldable elements.

➤ Editor: Show Folding Controls—By default, the folding controls (the plus and minus boxes) only appear when you hover your mouse over that part of the editor. If you prefer to have the folding controls always be visible, change this setting to "always."

➤ *Format Document, Format Selection*—These commands are used to reformat the document based on the formatter associated with the current language. Out of the box (which has become a very antiquated phrase), Visual Studio Code supports code formatting for JavaScript, TypeScript, JSON, C#, and HTML. But extensions are available on the Marketplace that support other languages.

Both of these commands run the current language's formatter on either the entire document or just the current selection.

➤ *Go Back, Go Forward*—Move the cursor to different positions, even if that position was in a different file. Go Back moves to the position you came from to get where you are. Go Forward moves to a position you were at prior to going back.

➤ *Go to Bracket*—Moves to the beginning or end of the current block.

➤ *Go to Last Edit Location*—Similar to Go Back and Go Forward, but it only stops at locations where you actually made changes.

➤ *Insert Line Above, Insert Line Below*—Add a blank line above and below the current line.

➤ *Move Line Up, Move Line Down*—Take the current line and moves it up (or down) by a line.

➤ *New Window*—Creates a new instance of Visual Studio Code. By default, you are on the welcome page and can open any project or workspace you desire.

➤ *Show All Commands*—Opens the Command Palette at the top of the IDE. The Command Palette is described in the "Command Palette" section in Chapter 2, "Exploring the User Interface."

➤ *Show Editor Context Menu*—This command is brilliant when it comes to keeping your hands on the keyboard. It shows the context menu for the editor as if you had right-clicked at the current cursor.

➤ *Show Hover*—Like the previous command, this is intended to truly allow you to work mouse-free. It shows what you would see if you hovered your mouse over the current cursor.

➤ *Shrink Selection*—Shrink Selection works in a similar manner to the Expand Selection command described earlier, except that instead of increasing the size of the selection, the command makes it smaller.

➤ *Soft Undo*—Consider this to be a stack of your cursor positions, with the most recent position on the top. With each subsequent execution of this command, your cursor will move to previous cursor positions.

➤ *Toggle Block Comment*—Wraps the current selection in the comment characters for the current language. Or, if the selection is currently commented, it removes the comment characters.

➤ *Toggle Line Comment*—Adds the comment character for the current language to the front of the line. Or, if the line is already commented, removes the comment.

➤ *Trigger Parameter Hints, Trigger Suggest*—These commands also fall into the category of keeping your hand away from the mouse. They trigger the parameter hints tooltip and the automatic suggestions. What you see with both of these commands is based on the current cursor position.

➤ *Trim Trailing White-space*—Removes any whitespace at the end of the current line.

Choosing Your Language

Visual Studio Code can edit many file types. Upon installation, editors are available for the following languages: JavaScript, JSON, HTML, CSS, TypeScript, Markdown, PowerShell, C++, Java, PHP, Python, Go, T-SQL, and C#. But beyond that, an active third-party ecosystem has contributed editors for many other languages. The Marketplace and how to add languages are discussed in Chapter 9, "Working with Extensions."

The language editor being used is determined by associating a file extension with a particular editor. If you have been editing files for a while, the list of default associations won't surprise you. For instance, `*.html` opens the HTML editor and `*.js` opens the JavaScript editor. But if you want to modify or change the association, you can do that through the File: Associations setting.

What is different about this setting, however, is that there is no interface within Visual Studio Code to make the changes. Instead, in the Settings tab is a link that opens the `settings.json` file and lets you edit the associations directly. For example, the following would associate `*.jsx` files with the JavaScript editor:

```
{
    "workbench.colorTheme": "Default Light+",
/* more settings */
    "file.associations": {
        "*.jsx": "javascript"
    }
}
```

Take note of the fact that the `settings.json` file is not just for file associations. It actually contains all of the custom settings that you have defined. The Settings tab is just the interface that allows you to easily modify the contents, but you can always access the file directly—the point being that as you update the file associations, take care not to remove or change other settings inadvertently.

You can add as many associations as you desire by adding more pairs of file extensions (using the glob pattern for wildcarding) and editor names. The only requirement is that you know the name of the editor. For a current list of known language strings, check out `https://code.visualstudio.com/docs/languages/identifiers#_known-language-identifiers`.

Formatting

Formatting text in various ways is a common function of text editors, and Visual Studio Code is no exception. One of the benefits of the extensibility that Visual Studio Code has is that it allows the editors themselves to implement the formatting, which makes sense. What component would know better how to format JavaScript/C#/PHP/Python/etc. than the editor that specializes in that language?

What Visual Studio Code brings to the formatting table is the ability to specify when the formatting is performed. Three options are available. The options are not mutually exclusive, so you can choose any, all, or none of them. They are, however, dependent on the editor having a formatter available, something that is not the case for every third-party editor:

➤ *Format on Paste*—Performs a format on the pasted content immediately after it has been pasted. This option requires that the editor have a formatter that supports formatting a range, which is to say that not every formatter is capable of formatting just a block of text. In some cases, it is only able to format the entire file, not just parts of it. If that's the case, this option isn't supported.

➤ *Format on Save*—Performs a format on the entire file when the file is saved. There is a separate option (Format on Save Timeout) that places a limit on how long the formatting takes before it is cancelled. The default timeout is 750 milliseconds. The idea here is to ensure that formatting doesn't prevent the save from taking place, because, except in cases that are difficult to imagine, saving the file is more important than formatting it.

➤ *Format on Type*—Performs a format on the line after it has been typed.

Code Writing Assistance

Settings are also available that control how the editor helps you to write code. From experience, whether these settings should be turned off or on is a very personal choice. If you peruse the forums looking for questions about how to adjust the default settings, you'll get a sense of how passionate people can be about, say, font color and kerning—the upshot being that it's important to know what the editor can do and how you can change it to fit your style.

With that in mind, what follows are some of the settings that are related to getting Visual Studio Code to help you write code:

➤ Editor: Auto Closing Brackets—Specifies whether the editor will automatically add a closing bracket when the user types an opening bracket. There is one option alongside the relatively obvious choices of "always" and "never"—whether the character to the right of the cursor after the opening bracket is typed is white-space to trigger the closing bracket. If this configuration is set to `beforeWhitespace`, an opening bracket typed immediately to the left of existing text will not generate a closing bracket. However, if you type an opening bracket and there is no character to the right (or it's a space character), the close bracket is automatically added. The other value for this setting, `languageDefined`, allows the editor for each language to determine the appropriate behavior.

➤ Editor: Auto Closing Quotes—Specifies whether the editor automatically adds a closing quote immediately after an opening quote is entered. Like the Auto Closing Brackets option, the following four choices are available:

➤ *Always*—Always add the closing quote.

➤ *Never*—Never add the closing quote.

➤ *Before White-space*—Add the closing quote only if there is white-space to the right of the cursor immediately after the opening quote was typed.

➤ *Language Defined*—Allow the editor for the language to determine the appropriate auto-close behavior.

➤ Editor: Auto Surround Selection—This setting definitely falls into the category of personal preference. The premise is that you select a block of text and then type one of the bounding characters (parentheses, brackets, quotes). When auto surround is turned on, the selection would be wrapped with the typed character. In other words, if you select TEST and type (, the result would be (TEST). Where this can become annoying is if you expected the keystroke to result in the selected text being deleted.

The default setting is to allow the language to define the behavior, so you get different results based on the type of file you have open. A couple of other settings are available that give you a little more control:

> ➤ *Brackets*—Only auto surround the selection when the boundary key is a bracket character. In this instance, *bracket* is defined as a square bracket, a curly brace, or a parenthesis.

> ➤ *Quotes*—Only auto surround the selection when the boundary key is a double or single quote.

> ➤ *Never*—Don't ever auto surround a selection.

➤ Editor: Line Numbers—The purpose of this setting is pretty straightforward. It determines whether there are line numbers to the left of the lines in the editor. However, a couple of values are a little out of the ordinary when it comes to configuring line numbers. The possible values are as follows:

> ➤ *Off*—No line numbers appear.

> ➤ *On*—Line numbers are placed to the left of each line. The first line in the file is considered to be line 1.

> ➤ *Relative*—Line numbers are placed to the left of each line, but the value is calculated as the number of lines to the current cursor position. So, for instance, both the line above and the line below the cursor position would be line 1.

> ➤ *Interval*—Line numbers are to the left of the line only every 10 lines. The exception is the number of the line with the cursor is also rendered.

➤ Editor: Mouse Wheel Zoom—This setting determines whether scrolling the mouse wheel, in conjunction with holding down the Ctrl key, causes the font size to grow and shrink. This setting is mentioned because the default is to have this setting turned off, which might be a little off-putting for Visual Studio users.

➤ Editor: Show Unused—Visual Studio Code has the ability to gray out code that is not being used. This is useful, especially if you're trying to refactor or clean up existing code. However, if you'd rather not have this functionality, you can turn it off by unchecking this configuration.

➤ Editor: Tab Completion—One of the powerful features of modern IDEs is automatic completion of partially entered commands. For instance, if you type the first couple of letters of a function name, IntelliSense displays a list of matching functions and you select the most appropriate one and use the Tab key to confirm your choice.

This configuration is used to turn on and off the tab completion functionality. As well, there is a third option, onlySnippets, which causes the tab completion to only work for code snippets and not method or variable names.

➤ Editor: Enable Trash—This setting controls what happens to a file when you delete it from within Visual Studio Code. By default, this setting is enabled, which means that deleted files are placed into the trash or Recycle Bin (depending on your OS). If this setting is unchecked, files deleted within Visual Studio Code are permanently deleted.

IntelliSense

IntelliSense is the collective name for a set of features that are related to code editing. It includes functions such as code completion, parameter information, quick information, and member lists.

The support for IntelliSense is pretty pervasive throughout Visual Studio Code. There is extensive support for TypeScript, JSON, HTML, CSS, SCSS, and Less with the initial installation. Beyond that, for any type of file there is support for word-based completions. This means that common words are immediately recognized, and options are provided to quickly enter the words. If you want more sophisticated IntelliSense capability, the number of extensions for different languages that are available in the Marketplace is very impressive. You can find details about how to locate and install these extensions in Chapter 9.

The features of IntelliSense are provided by a language service. This is code that runs in a separate process (so as to not slow down the editing process). As you type, information about the file and workspace are provided to this service. The service is then responsible for providing any information (like suggestions, parameters, and so on) that is appropriate.

Aside from just performance considerations, the context, semantics, and other analysis is very language-specific. With its own service, each language can focus on what it knows best. In addition, upgrading or installing new versions or languages is not only straightforward, but there is no concern that installing one language will break the functionality of another.

Method Info

You can use a number of different techniques to get information about a specific method. To start with, hover your mouse over a method name. After a brief period, a tooltip appears, as shown in Figure 4-19.

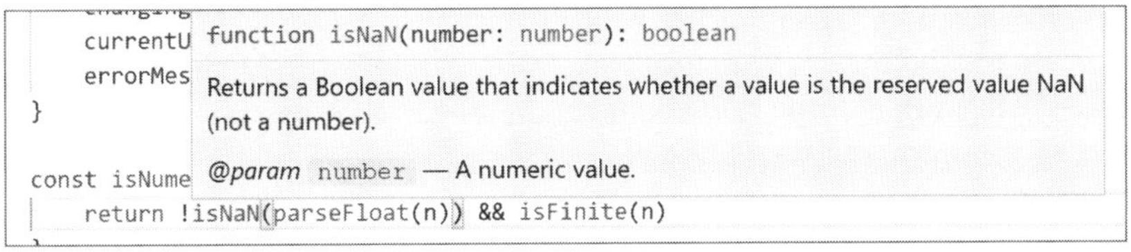

FIGURE 4-19

The tooltip contains information that is returned by the language service, so it's difficult to describe every possible combination. But in general, it includes the method's signature (including the data type for each parameter), the returned data type, and a brief description of what the method does.

If you move the cursor into the parameter list for a method, what you see in the tooltip changes slightly.

As you can see in Figure 4-20, the available information now focuses more on the parameters for the method. If the method takes more than one parameter, hovering over each of the parameter sections (delimited by a comma) displays the information about that parameter.

```
        changingPasswo  isNaN(number: number): boolean
        currentUser: n
        errorMessage:    A numeric value.
}
                         Returns a Boolean value that indicates whether a value is the
  const isNumeric =      reserved value NaN (not a number).
     return !isNaN(parseFloat(n)) && isFinite(n)
```

FIGURE 4-20

Completions

With your cursor at any position in your code, you can see a list of possible input options by using Ctrl+Space. The options in this list are called *completions* and you can see an example in Figure 4-21.

```
const isNumeric = (n) => {
    return !isNaN(parseFloat(n)) && isFinite(n)
}                       🟦 isNaN              function isNaN(number: number): boolea ×
                        ▣ isNumeric          n
const displayCu ≣ instanceof
    if (isNumer 🟦 isFinite                   Returns a Boolean value that indicates whether a
        return  abc isFinite                  value is the reserved value NaN (not a number).
    } else {    ▣ initialState
        return  [●] isSecureContext           @param number — A numeric value.
    }           [●] ProcessingInstruction
}               [●] SVGElementInstance
                [●] SVGElementInstanceList
```

FIGURE 4-21

The list of options appears in the drop-down. The list is composed of word completions that come from Visual Studio Code, inferred symbols, and global identifiers. This list is filtered based on the characters that you type, so you can get close to the desired input, and then use Enter or Tab to indicate your choices. For more information about a particular option, hover your mouse over the option and an information icon appears to the right. Clicking the icon displays detailed information about the variable or method (visible in Figure 4-21).

To the left of each item in the list is an icon that indicates the type of completion. Figure 4-22 shows the different icons (taken from the Visual Studio Code documentation).

Settings

A number of settings allow you to configure the behavior of IntelliSense. To understand the purpose of the first couple of settings, it helps to understand the concept of a commit character.

In the world of IntelliSense, a *commit character* is a character that causes a suggestion to be accepted. The default commit character for Visual Studio Code is a tab. However,

🟦	Methods, Functions and Constructors
◼	Variables and Fields
🔗	Classes
●○	Interfaces
{}	Modules
🔧	Properties and Attributes
🗐	Values and Enumerations
🗐	References
≣	Keywords
🗋	Global Identifiers
🎨	Colors
▫▫▫	Unit
▢	Snippet Prefixes
abc	Words
▲●	Miscellaneous

FIGURE 4-22

certain languages add other commit characters. For example, in JavaScript, a semicolon is also a commit character. The difference, in this case, is that not only does the semicolon accept a suggestion, but it also adds a semicolon to the file.

The Editor: Accept Suggestion On Commit Character setting is used to turn on or off the use of commit characters to accept suggestions.

Along with the Tab character, the Editor: Accept Suggestion On Enter setting is used to add Enter as a commit character. What's interesting about this setting is that not only can you turn this on and off, but there is also a Smart option. In this latter case, the Enter key may or may not be interpreted as a commit character depending on the situation.

The Editor: Quick Suggestions setting is used to determine when suggestions will actually appear. There is no user interface in Visual Studio Code for this setting. Instead, it is modified directly in the JSON file. Following is an example of this setting:

```
"editor.quickSuggestions": {
  "other": true,
  "comments": false,
  "strings": false
}
```

This setting contains three attributes. The Comments and the Strings settings determine if suggestions appear when you are typing within a comment or within a string. You'll notice that those settings are set to false by default, because it might feel a little unusual to have a suggestion for words or methods appear while typing within a string. The Other setting, set to true by default, indicates that suggestions appear whenever you are typing outside a comment or a string.

Find and Replace

Searching across all of the files and folders in a workspace is covered in the "Search" section in Chapter 3. The techniques that relate to specifying case sensitivity and the use of regular expressions that applied to file search also apply to searching and replacing within a file.

First, to invoke the find functionality at a file level, use the Find command (default is Ctrl+F). This causes a small pane, shown in Figure 4-23, to appear in the top right of the current editor.

FIGURE 4-23

The basic approach is to type the text you want to find into the text box. The number of matches that are in the file appears to the right of the text box and the editor moves to the closest match moving forward through the file. Figure 4-23 shows seven matches in total and the closest match was the second of those seven. The two arrows at the right side of the pane are used to navigate to the next and previous matches. This process is circular, in that if you're at the seventh match and click the Next arrow, you will move to the first match in the file.

Inside the text box are three icons that change the characteristics of the find process. The first icon toggles on and off the case sensitivity of the search. The second icon toggles on and off the whole-word capabilities of the search. In other words, when on, the only matches will be if the text is an entire word as determined by using the word bounding characters (such as spaces, punctuation, brackets, and so on). The final icon toggles on and off regular expression searching. When this option is on, the content of the text box needs to be a valid regular expression before the searching is performed.

The only icons left undescribed to this point are the last two to the right. The X icon at the far right is used to clear the contents of the text box. The second icon from the right is used to toggle the selection bounding functionality. If the editor has a selection active and this icon is toggled on, the find will only be performed within the selection.

The Find pane also takes part in the replace functionality. You can perform a replace by either using the triangle to open the lower portion of the pane or executing the Replace command (Ctrl+H by default). Figure 4-24 shows the Replace pane.

FIGURE 4-24

The lower portion of the pane includes a second text box. This is the text that the contents of the first text box will be replaced with. To the right of the text box are a couple of icons that control the scope of the replacement. The first icon (on the left) will replace only the next match. The second icon replaces all of the matches.

Minimap

The idea for a Minimap is not unique to Visual Studio Code, although the name itself might not be familiar to you. An example of a Minimap is shown in Figure 4-25.

The area on the right of Figure 4-25, immediately to the left of the scroll bar, is the Minimap. It's part of the scroll bar, in that it can be used to move up and down through the code. However, the content is definitely not the plain gray that makes up the regular scroll bar. Instead, it contains a representation of the code. Depending on a configuration setting, this representation is either the code file in a really, really, tiny font or just colored shapes that mimic the shape of the file's contents. The purpose of the Minimap is to allow you to more quickly find the place you want in your code file.

FIGURE 4-25

You can customize the appearance of the Minimap within the IDE. The settings that are used to accomplish this are as follows:

➤ Minimap: Enabled—If checked, the Minimap appears. Otherwise, it's just the regular scroll bar.

➤ Minimap: Max Column—Specifies the maximum size of the Minimap column. This setting keeps the area from being overwhelmingly large if the file lines were long.

➤ Minimap: Render Characters—When checked, the tiny font is used in the Minimap. Otherwise, the colored boxes are used.

➤ Minimap: Show Slider—In Figure 4-25 you can see that a section of the Minimap is a darker color. This area indicates the portion of the code file that is currently visible on the screen. This configuration allows the shaded area to appear either always or only when you mouse over the Minimap.

➤ Minimap: Side—Determines which side of the editor the Minimap appears on. The choices are either Right (the default) or Left.

Code Snippets

The purpose of code snippets is to help speed the writing of commonly used blocks of code. When used properly, it can even help to maintain consistency of style throughout a team.

A code snippet is a template of commonly used code patterns. For instance, most languages would have a loop or a conditional template. As a coder, you would select the loop template and it would add the basic syntactical structure of the loop to your file. Then you could modify the structure with the specifics for your situation.

In Visual Studio Code, any available snippets are included with the IntelliSense options. They are mixed with the keywords and methods in the list of options choices. You can tell which option is a snippet by the icon that appears. In Figure 4-22, the square with the dotted bottom indicates the snippets.

Practically, including snippets with other IntelliSense options means that, as you start to type, the snippets that match your text are displayed automatically. To insert the snippet, select your choice using the mouse, or use the Tab or Enter key. If you hover the mouse over the snippet in the list of options, a description of the snippet, along with the code that will be inserted, is visible.

The snippets are available in three different categories: global, language-specific, and project-specific. Ultimately, this means that each editor is going to expose its own set of code snippets. It also means that describing every possible snippet is not practical. However, to give you a sense of how the template works, consider the snippet shown in Figure 4-26.

FIGURE 4-26

Two tokens in this code snippet need to be replaced. They are array and element, and both of them are highlighted once the snippet has been inserted into your code. The first token in the snippet is selected and if you start typing, the token will be replaced by what you type. When you have finished the first token, pressing the Tab key moves the cursor to the next token. One of the conveniences of a snippet is that if the same token name appears more than once in a snippet, replacing any of the tokens will change all of them.

You can create your own snippets through Visual Studio Code. Choose File ⇨ Preferences ⇨ User Snippets to start the process. The pane shown in Figure 4-27 appears.

This pane allows you to specify the location and scope of the new snippet. The top two options add the snippet to the global scope or just for the current project. The remaining options associate the snippet with a particular language.

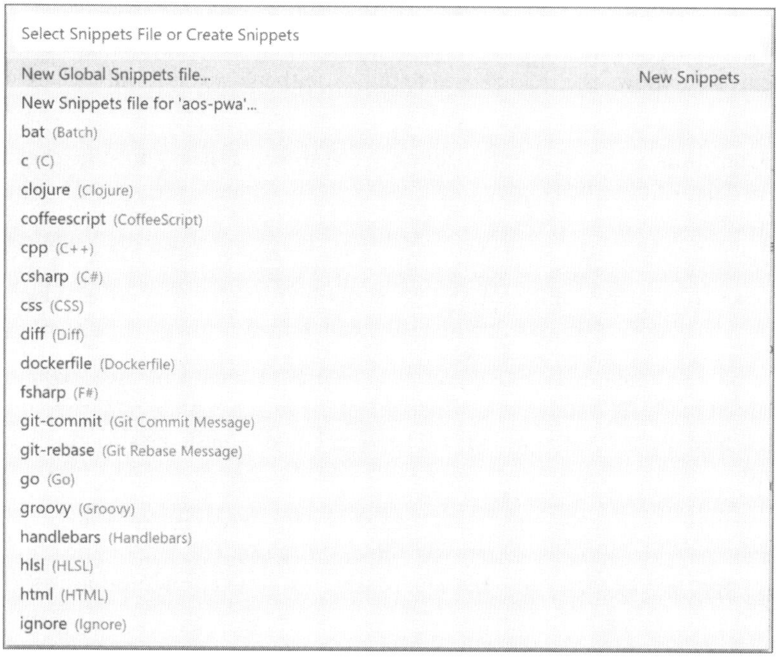

FIGURE 4-27

The format of each snippet is a JSON file. Following is an example for a JavaScript snippet:

```
"Print to console": {
    "prefix": "log",
    "body": [
        "console.log('$1');"
    ],
    "description": "Log output to console"
}
```

In this example, the name of the snippet is `Print to console`. The prefix, `log` in the example, defines the set of characters that IntelliSense uses to determine when the snippet should be displayed. The `description` attribute is just as you would expect—the description of the snippet. Finally, the `body` attribute defines the actual code for the snippet itself. Notice that the body is actually a JSON array. Each element in the array corresponds to a line within the output.

The tokens in the snippet are defined using a $n notation. So the first token is $1, the second token is $2, and so on. If you want to have the snippet use names as tokens, they are formatted using a bracketed notation. So the body could be rewritten as:

```
"body": [
    "console.log('${1:message}');"
],
```

Now in the snippet the placeholder `message` appears in the inserted code.

The final thing to be aware of is that the $0 token has a special purpose. It is used to define the placement for the cursor after the snippet has been inserted. So you could, for example, define the body of a loop as follows:

```
"body": [
    "for (const ${2:item} of ${1:array}) {",
    "\t$0",
    "}"
],
```

Now, after the snippet tokens have been replaced, the cursor will be positioned inside the loop, preceded by a tab character.

Multiple Cursors

Visual Studio Code supports the addition and operation of multiple cursors. This is exactly what it sounds like. You can add more than one cursor to your editor. Then, as you use the keyboard to move around (with, for example, the arrow keys) or select text, each of the cursors will act as the starting point for whatever command you execute.

For example, if you have two cursors in your file, and you use the Select Word command (Ctrl+D is the default), a word is selected at both of the cursor locations.

There is a setting (Editor: Multi Cursor Modifier) that controls how multiple cursors are added to your editor. To create more than one cursor, you hold a specific key down when you click in each location. The default is the Alt key (or the Options key in macOS). The other choice is to use the Ctrl key (or the Command key in macOS).

Auto Save

While Visual Studio Code supports autosaving of changes, the feature is turned off by default. This might come as a bit of a surprise to Visual Studio users, but it makes sense in the context of editing for web applications, where it's common to have file changes trigger a rebuilding of the application.

Through a setting named Files: Auto Save, it is possible to turn auto saving on. Three options are available for when a modified file will be saved:

➤ *After Delay*—The file is saved after a period of time that starts with the moment the file is modified. How long that period is can be configured using the Auto Save Delay value (described in a bit). If subsequent changes are made before the Auto Save Delay value has expired, the timer is reset and the waiting begins again.

➤ *On Focus Change*—The file is saved when the focus moves out of the editor for that file.

➤ *On Window Change*—The file is saved when Visual Studio Code loses focus.

You can also control the frequency with which a file is saved. The Files: Auto Save Delay setting defines the number of milliseconds after a file change before the file will be saved. This value is only used if the value of the Auto Save configuration is set to After Delay.

Hot Exit

The concept of a hot exit is an interesting one. Its utility is best experienced rather than just described, because, when you get used to it, it's quite natural.

As you work on a file, Visual Studio Code takes a backup on a regular basis. In the unlikely event that Visual Studio Code crashes, when you relaunch the application, the backups are used to restore the file to the edited state it was in.

However, a hot exit takes this a step further by keeping the backups even if Visual Studio Code exits normally. So rather than asking if you want to save all of your changed files on exit, it just stores the backup. When you next open Visual Studio Code, all of the changes are still there. And if you now close the file without saving, any changes you made would be lost (exactly as if you hadn't closed Visual Studio Code in the interim). In other words, the normal editing flow continues even across different sessions.

Three options are available for the Files: Hot Exit setting. First, you can turn it off completely (the value is `off`). This means that you get prompted to save files when you exit. The default setting (the value is `onExit`) is to trigger a saving of the backups when the last folder open in Visual Studio Code is closed. The last setting is `onExitAndWindowClose`. This saves backups not only when the last open folder is closed, but also any time a folder is closed. This feature is useful only in situations where your workspace has multiple folders in it.

EDITOR SETTINGS

By this point, not only in the chapter, but also the book, you should be aware of the range of configuration options that Visual Studio Code provides. The editor is no exception. This section discusses some of the most useful settings that relate to the editor, but which didn't neatly fit into the other topics in this chapter.

To start, you can access the main Settings page through the gear icon that appears in the bottom left of the Visual Studio Code window. Clicking the icon displays a context menu, and clicking the Settings option opens the Settings editor (Figure 4-28).

It's also possible to get to the Settings editor by using the File ➪ Preferences ➪ Settings menu option. Or, you can use the Command Palette (View ➪ Command Palette) and enter **Preferences: Edit User Settings**.

Settings are persisted in two separate blocks: User Settings and Workspace Settings. You can see these two items as tab headers immediately below the Search Settings text box. The list of possible settings is the same for each block. That is to say 522 settings are available both as user settings and as workspace settings. The difference is the scope at which the setting is applied:

➤ *User Settings*—Applied to any instance of Visual Studio Code that you open.

➤ *Workspace Settings*—Applied to the specific workspace that is being opened. If multiple workspaces are open, a scope will be visible for each workspace.

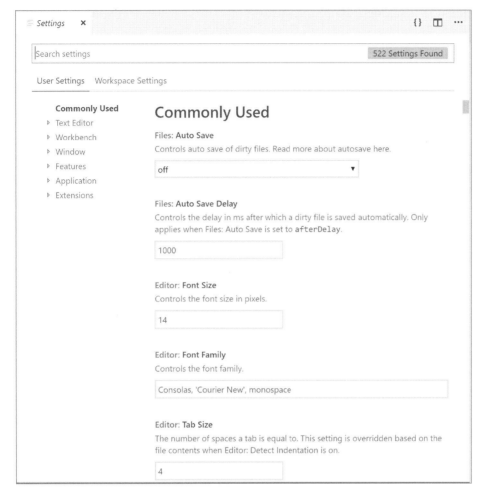

FIGURE 4-28

In order for the scope of the groups of settings to be consistent with these definitions, any configuration value in the workplace settings overrides the same configuration in the user settings.

The settings are divided into different categories. This appears in a tree navigation control on the left side of the Settings editor. Expanding any one of the categories displays a number of subcategories. When either a category or a subcategory is selected, the settings for that group are displayed on the right.

In addition, and differently than many tree-like navigations, you can move from group to group of the setting items by using the scroll bar on the right. As you scroll up and down, the category and subcategory on the left will change. So you can actually scroll through all of the setting items without going through the categories:

➤ Editor: Font Size—Sets the size of the characters in the editor. The value is specified as pixels; this is only the default value. For any editor, you're able to increase the size of the font using the Editor Font Zoom In and Editor Font Zoom Out (or Editor Font Zoom Reset) commands. These commands are available from the Command Palette (View ➪ Command Palette from the menu).

➤ Editor: Font Family—Determines the font used to display the content of files in the editor. The value here can be a comma-separated list of font families. The subsequent values are fallback fonts. If, when a project is opened on different platforms, a particular font is not available, it falls back to the next family in the list.

➤ Editor: Tab Size—The number of spaces that are the equivalent of a tab character. This is used to specify the indentation of code files using the Tab key. If Detect Indentation is turned on for the editor, the calculated value (based on the file contents) overrides this configuration value.

➤ Editor: Render White-space—This option controls how white-space appears within the editor. By default, it isn't rendered, so code appears as it does in the image on the left of Figure 4-29. However, if you change the setting, all of a sudden the spaces get rendered as dots, as shown in the image on the right of Figure 4-29.

This setting has three values:

➤ *None*—Spaces are not rendered at all (the left image of Figure 4-29). This is the default setting.

➤ *Boundary*—All spaces are rendered as dots, except for the single space that appears between words. This setting is visible in the image on the right of Figure 4-29.

➤ *All*—All spaces are rendered as dots, including between words.

```
function TabContainer({ children }) {
    return (
        <Typography component="div">
            {children}
        </Typography>
    );
}
```

```
function TabContainer({ children }) {
····return (
········<Typography component="div">
············{children}
········</Typography>
····);
}
```

FIGURE 4-29

➤ Editor: Cursor Style—Controls the size and shape of the cursor within the editor. Three basic styles are available: line, block, and underline. In addition, each of the styles has a regular and a thin rendering. As a result, you have a total of six different styles to choose from.

➤ Editor: Insert Spaces—When this setting is checked, spaces are inserted into the file editor when a Tab key is pressed. If unchecked, a tab is inserted. The default is to insert spaces and if the Detect Indentation setting is true, the behavior is determined by analyzing the file's contents.

➤ Editor: Word Wrap—Determines when a line of text will be wrapped. The default value is to not wrap at all. This means that a long line of text is only visible by scrolling the viewport. However, when you turn word wrap on, a number of different options are available that work in conjunction with the Word Wrap Column setting. The following are the possible settings:

  ➤ *Off*—No wrapping at all.

  ➤ *On*—Lines are wrapped at the edge of the viewport.

  ➤ *Word Wrap Column*—Lines are wrapped at the column specified in the Word Wrap Column setting. So if the Word Wrap Column setting is 40, the lines are wrapped at the fortieth column.

  ➤ *Bounded*—Lines are wrapped at the lesser of the Word Wrap Column setting and the width of the viewport.

➤ Editor: Word Wrap Column—Specifies the column at which lines will be wrapped, depending on the value of the Word Wrap configuration setting.

SUMMARY

Learning the capabilities of an editor is crucial to being effective in that editor. Given that Visual Studio Code has editing as its core function, the plethora of built-in features and functionality shouldn't be surprising, You can see that you have a wide variety of ways to configure the editor to fit your own coding style.

This chapter looked at the approach that Visual Studio Code takes to editing, the various features that are implemented in the editor, and the many different ways you have to tailor the editing function to your personal preferences.

5

Integrating with Source Control

WHAT'S IN THIS CHAPTER?

➤ Understanding how to use Git from within Visual Studio Code

➤ Adding additional source control providers

To be able to provide a complete end-to-end developer experience, the code editor being used should integrate with source control providers. While there might be some developers for whom this is not an absolute requirement, few professional developers do not use some form of source control in their day-to-day efforts. The ability to work with source control without moving to a different interface is a productivity boost. Fortunately, Visual Studio Code includes built-in integration with Git and access to a wide variety of other source control tools through readily available extensions.

SOURCE CONTROL MANAGEMENT

It seems almost quaint to look back a couple of decades to how large software projects were created. In particular, how the coordination of editing multiple files by multiple developers simultaneously were managed. Yes, there was a time before source control tools were sophisticated—and it wasn't pretty.

But modern software development needs modern source control tools. They are an integral part of any large-scale (and most small- and medium-scale) development efforts. In an ideal world, the tool that you use to write code will seamlessly integrate into your source control environment. And, while the world itself might not be ideal, at least if you're using Visual Studio Code, your ability to participate in source control management remains intact.

Visual Studio Code is tightly integrated with built-in support for Git. Extensions are available in the Marketplace that support Perforce, SVN, and Mercurial, to name just a few. But even beyond support for these source control providers, Visual Studio Code has some features that can be useful, especially if you're working in an environment that has multiple "standard" sound control tools.

The starting point for any of the source control tools (other than Git) is to install the necessary extension. The process to do this is covered in Chapter 9, "Working with Extensions." Once the provider is available, you can pick and choose the one you're going to work with quite easily. Start by clicking the Source Control icon in the Activity Bar. This displays the Source Control view. Both of these are shown in Figure 5-1, with the Source Control icon being the third one from the top that looks like a Y (or, more appropriately, a fork).

If you right-click the Source Control label at the top, the context menu allows you to select from the available Source Control Providers or just access any of the ones you have configured for the current workspace. If you choose to show the list of Source Control Providers, you'll see a list similar to that shown in Figure 5-2.

From this list you have a number of different options available, all of which relate to source control, naturally.

First, the Refresh icon at the right (the circle of arrows) is used to synchronize your local repository with the remote one. Click the icon and the synchronization will start, or you might receive a dialog asking you to confirm the synchronization. That depends on the configuration for your repository.

FIGURE 5-1

Clicking the branch (named "master" in Figure 5-2) displays a pane that provides a few more few options. While the specifics of the list depend on the provider, they are all related to branching. Figure 5-3 shows the choices if you are connected to a Git repository.

The first two choices in the pane allow you to create a new branch. In both cases, you are prompted to provide the name of the branch. In the second option, you must also choose the branch from which the new one is created.

The other options on this pane depend on the contents of the local and remote repository. It is a list of the branches that are available, both locally and remotely. By clicking a branch, you initiate the process of checking out that branch. Whether this works or

FIGURE 5-2

whether you receive additional messages depends on the state of your current repository. For instance, you can't perform a `git checkout` if changes in the current branch would be overwritten. The best way to think about this option is to be aware that what you see in Figure 5-3 is just a user interface on top of the `git checkout` command. That means that any restrictions that would be applied to that command are also applicable here.

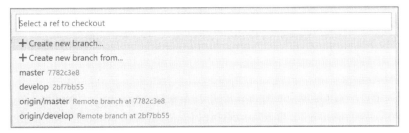

FIGURE 5-3

If you click the name of the branch, you open that particular branch in the Source Control view (as seen in Figure 5-4). Now the possibilities expand by an order of magnitude. The possibilities for Git repositories are covered in the next section.

FIGURE 5-4

USING GIT

While support for Git is built into Visual Studio Code, it leverages the Git installation on your machine in order to work properly (which, of course, implies that you need to have Git installed in order for Visual Studio Code to work with it). If it is not already installed, you can find the package and instructions to install it at `https://git-scm.com/download`. Here you can choose the appropriate platform (Git is supported on Linux, macOS, and Windows) and find links to additional resources if you want to learn more about Git.

As you configure Git for the first time, you might see a prompt in the bottom right of Visual Studio Code asking if the project should periodically perform an automatic fetch. The reason for doing this fetch is purely cosmetic. By performing a fetch, Visual Studio Code is able to accurately maintain the number of incoming and outgoing commits. Whether autofetch is turned on or off doesn't impact any functionality in Visual Studio Code beyond those values. So the choice as to whether this is turned on is yours, with complete awareness of the ramifications. If you want to change the behavior in the future, you can modify it through the Git: Autofetch setting. You can configure the frequency of the fetch through the Git: Autofetch Period setting.

As a word of caution, there have been reports that the automatic fetch will sometimes cause Git to request that you enter your credentials for the repository. That happens because of a situation where the initial fetch is being performed prior to the credentials being available. If that happens, one of the more reliable fixes is to disable automatic fetch and live with inaccurate commit counts.

Cloning a Repository

The starting point for working with Git is frequently to clone an existing repository. While there isn't much in the way of user interface to support this within Visual Studio Code, it is still possible to perform that task. From the Command Palette (View ➪ Command Palette), issue the Git: Clone command. You are prompted for the URL associated with the repository and the directory into which you want the local version of the repository to be placed.

Staging and Committing

As you make and save changes to the files in your workspace, the Source Control pane is updated accordingly. Figure 5-5 illustrates the pane after a single file has been modified.

First, notice that the Source Control icon has a number in a badge. This is the number of files that have been changed. The list of the files that have changed (but not yet staged) appears below the Changes title. As the mouse hovers over each file, three icons appear. These icons allow you to manipulate the file within source control.

The first icon (the document with an arrow at the top) is used to open the changed file. The second icon (the undo arrow) is used to discard any changes. This means that the file as it currently exists in your repository will replace the file. All changes will be lost. The third icon (the plus sign) is used to add the file to the staged list.

FIGURE 5-5

Within Git, committing a set of changes is typically a two-stage process. First, the files you want to include in the commit are staged. Then the staged files are committed. Putting a file into a staged state doesn't mean that you can't continue to change it. You can. Any changes you make are included when the commit takes place. All "being staged" indicates is that the file is ready to be part of a changeset.

You have several ways to stage a file in Visual Studio Code. You can right-click the file and choose Stage Changes in the context menu, you can click the plus icon that appears when your mouse hovers over the file, or, when your mouse hovers over the Changes label, you can click the plus icon to add all of the changed files to staging. When you have files in staging, the Changes label appears as a separate header, as shown in Figure 5-6.

FIGURE 5-6

When the time comes to commit the staged files, two parts of Figure 5-6 are of interest. To start, you use the text box at the top (with the Message interior label) to provide the commit message. A message must be provided before you can complete the commit. You complete the commit by clicking the checkmark at the top right of the pane or by using Ctrl+Enter.

Visual Studio Code doesn't require that you go through the two steps in order to commit files. The Message text box and the ability to commit always exists once any file has been modified. If you have staged files, executing a commit will only operate against the staged files. However, if you haven't staged any files, executing a commit will operate on *all* changed files.

Branches

Creating a branch in Git is both a commonly used function and also intended to be quick. The ability to quickly create and destroy branches is one of the key advantages over other source control environments, not to mention being able to switch between branches with speed. Visual Studio Code fully supports this important part of a developer's workflow.

Creating and switching between branches (known as "checking out a branch" in Git parlance) is available through the same interface. You have two ways to get started. The first is by clicking the branch name in the bottom left of Visual Studio Code. This causes the pane shown in Figure 5-7 to appear.

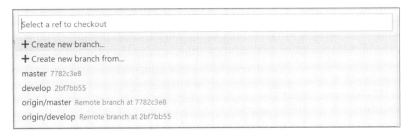

FIGURE 5-7

Within this pane, you have three main choices. You can switch to a different local branch by clicking the name of the desired branch. You can switch to a remote branch (and, if it doesn't already exist locally, add it to your local repository) by clicking the remote branch name.

The more complex tasks, at least from a user-interface perspective, is the creation of new branches. Figure 5-7 shows two options: Create New Branch and Create New Branch From. Both of these will create a new branch. The difference lies in the relationship between the new branch and an existing branch.

In Git, there is a concept called a "tracking branch." This is where one branch has a direct relationship with another branch. The relationship takes the form of automatically knowing where a pull will come from (refreshing one branch with the contents of another) or where a push will go (sending the changes from one branch to another). It's not a requirement that any particular branch track another branch. It's just that the flow of moving commits from branch to branch is made a lot simpler if they do.

Regardless of which Create New Branch option you choose, the first step is to provide the name for the new branch. You do this through a pane that appears at the top of the IDE. Once you have entered the name, press the Enter key to confirm the name. If you use the Create New Branch option, a new branch is created with that name and you're ready to go. If you use the Create New Branch From option, the screen in Figure 5-8 appears.

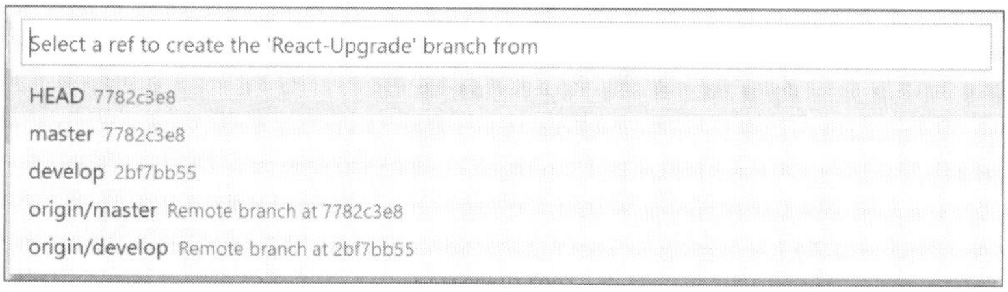

FIGURE 5-8

Here you can select the existing branch you want to use as the basis for the new branch. The list contains all of the local and remote branches, along with a branch called HEAD. The HEAD branch represents the last commit you made within your current branch. Select the branch you want to use, and the new branch will be created. In addition, that branch will be checked out, so that the name appears in the lower-left corner of the IDE.

Working with the Tracking Branch

When you have a tracking branch for your current branch (also known as an *upstream link*), a number of other functions are available to you. Specifically, you can push, pull, sync, and fetch from the tracking branch. Basically, the purpose of these operations are as follows:

➤ *Pull*—Takes any changes from the tracking branch and updates the current branch with them.

➤ *Push*—Takes any changes from the current branch and updates the tracking branch with them.

➤ *Sync*—Synchronizes the current branch and the remote branch. It accomplishes this by performing a pull followed by a push.

➤ *Fetch*—Downloads the most recent changes to the tracking branch without actually applying them to your local branch. This is so that you can see what other people have been working on within the tracking branch. Within Visual Studio Code, it is used to update the information that appears in the version control portion of the Status Bar (at the bottom left).

You have two different ways to execute these commands from within Visual Studio Code. In the Source Control view, clicking the ellipsis displays a context menu that includes the Git commands that are supported. Figure 5-9 shows the menu.

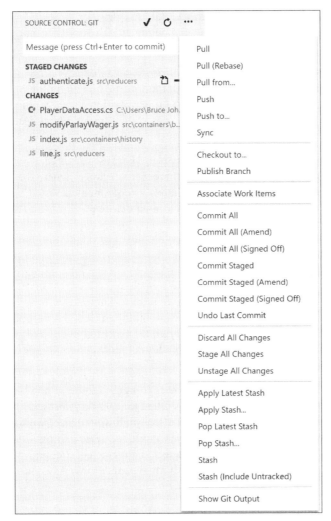

FIGURE 5-9

At the top of the context menu, you can see a number of different flavors of pulling and pushing. The bare options (Pull, Push) are used to perform the pull or the push against the tracked branch. The Pull From and Push To options allow you to specify the branch against which the operation is performed. You can use this not only if your local branch isn't tracking a different branch, but even if it is. The Pull (Rebase) is a specific kind of pull that is designed to "clean up" the history of the repository. Whether or not a pull rebase should be commonly used is a subject of deep philosophical debate and well beyond the scope of this book. Just be aware that it's available if you need it.

The other way to perform these commands is through the Command Palette (View ⇨ Command Palette). Once there, type in **Git** to see the complete list of Git-related commands. Notice that many of them mirror the list shown in Figure 5-9, including Pull, Push, and Sync.

The fetch is a bit of a different animal. Since its purpose is mostly informational, it doesn't have a place in Figure 5-9. Instead, it is executed only on demand (through the Command Palette) or through the autofetch setting. Keep in mind that the purpose of fetch (at least within Visual Studio Code) is to update the Status Bar at the bottom left. As such, you can easily do without a fetch. And, indeed, automatically fetching is turned off (in the most recent versions) by default.

One of the reasons why the default is off is because of a recurring problem. Because the fetch is being performed against a repository that frequently requires credentials, there were instances where the developer was being prompted for the Git credentials almost immediately after launching Visual Studio Code. This was a timing issue (internally, the fetch was being performed before the Git login) and a successful solution was to turn the automatic fetch setting to off.

Merge Conflicts

As you work with remote branches, situations arise where the remote branch and your local branch are going to be in conflict. What this means is that both branches have files in common that have been changed. It could be that two independent parts of the same file are modified (such as methods being added), or it could be that two developers added a different import statement at the top of the file. Regardless of the cause, if your current branch and the remote branch both have changes in them, they are considered to be in conflict.

When you perform a pull, Git recognizes that there is a conflict and tries to figure out how best to handle it. In many cases, the changes are different enough (such as when independent methods have been added) that Git can merge the two versions of the file successfully. However, there will be instances where the changes to the files (two import statements at the top of the file) are recognized as being in semantically similar locations. In this situation, Git has detected a merge conflict and the file in question is marked so that the different conflicting blocks are both available for review. As you might expect, having different blocks of code (especially with the boundary delimiters used by Git) added to a file impacts the execution of the code in a negative manner. The trick is how to identify these blocks and resolve the conflicts quickly and easily.

To start with, when merge conflicts exist, the Source Control pane lets you know (see Figure 5-10).

Any of the files that have existing merge conflicts appear in the section marked Merge Changes. The C to the right of the file and the icons indicates that there are still conflicts in the file. If you hover over the C, the tooltip indicates not just the full path to the file, but the type of conflict.

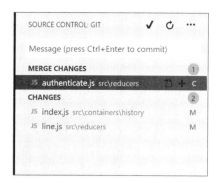

FIGURE 5-10

If you click the Open File icon (the document icon with the arrow at the top), the file is opened. All of the sections that are in conflict are highlighted with color (Figure 5-11).

```
Accept Current Change | Accept Incoming Change | Accept Both Changes | Compare Changes
<<<<<<< HEAD (Current Change)
    userId: null,
    password: null,
=======
    password: '',
    userId: '',
>>>>>>> c5a6a41552ab86a69b736404ea33e3b40052c5ea (Incoming Change)
```

FIGURE 5-11

At the top (in green, in the real world) are your current changes. At the bottom (in blue) are the changes being pulled from the remote branch. These are labeled as the Incoming Changes.

Across the top of this section of code are choices to address the conflict. They are:

➤ *Accept Current Change*—The section marked as Current Change is kept in the file, while the section marked as Incoming Change is deleted.

➤ *Accept Incoming Change*—The opposite result, where the Current Change is discarded, and the Incoming Change is kept.

➤ *Accept Both Changes*—Both changes are kept, with the Current Change positioned before the Incoming Change in the file.

➤ *Compare Changes*—Displays a screen where the current and incoming changes can be compared side-by-side (see Figure 5-12).

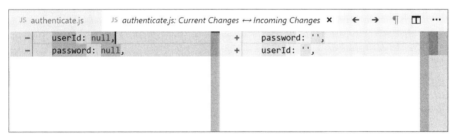

FIGURE 5-12

Though this diff view is generated within the context of Git, the same functionality is available between any two files. In the Explorer, you can right-click a file and set it to be part of a comparison. Then right-click a second file and use the context menu to initiate the comparison. This process is discussed in detail in the "Project View" section of Chapter 3, "Files and Folders and Projects (Oh My)."

> **NOTE** *As of this writing, no three-way diff merge functionality is available within Visual Studio Code. There have been discussions among the development team to add such functionality, but no plans have been announced.*

Miscellaneous Support

Visual Studio Code provides first-class integration with Git. As a result, there are a number of other areas where the two can work together, which can give you a better look at what Visual Studio Code is executing, as well as allowing Git to use Visual Studio Code directly.

Git Output

As you might have guessed, the different user interface elements that have been discussed in this chapter will ultimately result in the execution of Git commands. If you're interested (or you're trying to figure out why something isn't working), being able to see the commands that were executed is handy. The Output window provides that view.

Open the Output window using the View ⇨ Output command. A window similar to Figure 5-13 appears.

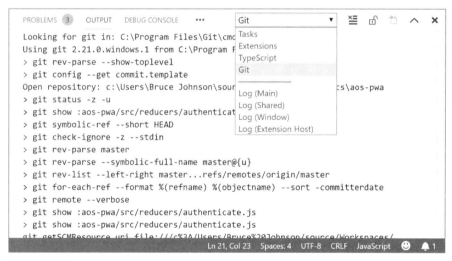

FIGURE 5-13

From the drop-down list at the top of the window, select the Git option. This shows the different Git commands that have been executed, along with their output. If there has been a problem, you're likely to find it here.

Default Git Editor

Visual Studio Code supports being opened as an editor from the command line. Actually, Visual Studio Code supports a wide variety of command-line options, but from the perspective of being the Git editor, launching the editor from the command line is sufficient.

Before Visual Studio Code can be the Git editor, you need to ensure that the executable is in your path. For Linux and Windows, you have that option as part of the installation process. For macOS, from the Command Palette, execute the command **Shell Command: Install 'Code' command in path**.

Now that Visual Studio Code can be launched from any command line, you can configure Git to use it. From Git Bash (or any other Git-enabled command line), execute the command **git config --global core.editor "code --wait"**. Now the configuration is complete.

While not a requirement, you might find it useful to add a **--new-window** option to the config command. This will cause a new instance of Visual Studio Code to be opened when triggered by Git (as opposed to utilizing the instance that you might currently be using).

Git Diff Tool

You can also configure Visual Studio Code to be the diff tool for Git. The starting steps are the same as for the Git editor configuration; that is, Visual Studio Code needs to be available from the command line. But once the executable is found in your PATH variable, the steps to configure are a little different.

To open the Git configuration file, execute the command **git config --global -e** from a command line. This will launch Visual Studio Code (presuming that it's the default editor). In the configuration file, add the following section.

```
[diff]
    tool = default-difftool
[difftool "default-difftool"]
    cmd = code --wait --diff $LOCAL $REMOTE
```

Save the file, and now Visual Studio Code will be used to perform the differencing for Git.

OTHER SCMs

As mentioned earlier in this chapter, there is support through the Marketplace for other source control management. In other words, while Git support is built into Visual Studio Code, there is also support for a Source Control API that allows third-party developers to integrate source control features into their extensions.

To see the different SCM extensions that are available, launch the Extensions pane, either through the Activity Bar, the View ⇨ Extensions menu item, or the Extensions option on the Gear context menu (also in the Activity Bar). Figure 5-14 shows the extensions that are visible when you use SCM as the search criteria.

FIGURE 5-14

You'll notice that some popular choices, like SVN, Perforce, Mercurial, and Clear Case are on that list, and some (Azure Repos being one) aren't in this list because SCM isn't a keyword for the extension. There are many different source control managers that are supported by Visual Studio Code. Finding them just might require a bit of searching.

To get access to the SCM, the first step is to install the extension. Then, in all likelihood, the extension will need to be configured. The configuration information and the flow are going to be different for each one. To give you a sense of what it could be like, the following section looks at the installation and configuration of the Azure Repos extension. Given the nature of SCMs, it's likely that there will be a great deal of similarity with it and any of the other options.

Installing the Extension

The first step in the process is to install the selection. In the Extensions pane, enter search criteria of **Azure Repo**. In the list that appears, choose the Azure Repos extension. Click the green Install button at the bottom right of the extension item to install the extension.

Once the extension has been installed (which shouldn't be more than a couple of minutes), a notification appears at the bottom of the IDE (Figure 5-15).

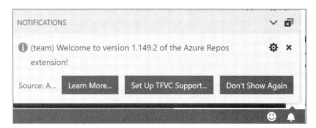

FIGURE 5-15

The Set Up TFVC Support button on this notification can be used to initiate the configuration. Or, more precisely, clicking on the button causes your default browser to appear, with a web page that describes how to configure TFVC (Team Foundation Version Control).

Configuring the Extension

To access your repositories in Azure DevOps, you need to have a personal access token (PAT). When you first connect to a TFVC repository, you will be prompted in a pane at the top of Visual Studio Code to choose the method by which you want to provide the PAT. Figure 5-16 shows this pane.

FIGURE 5-16

Two methods are available, described colloquially as the current experience and the new experience. If you choose the current experience, you'll see a pane into which the PAT must be entered (Figure 5-17).

FIGURE 5-17

Of course, the challenge is how to generate that PAT. You can find the instructions to do so at `https://aka.ms/qtgzt4`. Once you have the PAT and copy it into the text box, press Enter to complete the configuration process.

If you select the new experience, the process is a little smoother (or at least has fewer steps). The new experience starts with the pane shown in Figure 5-18.

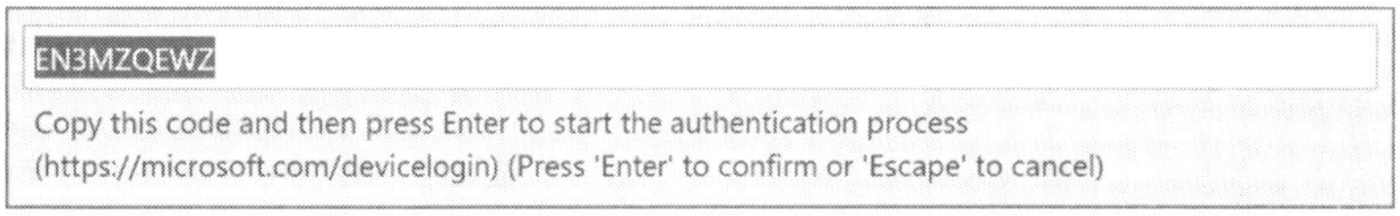

EN3MZQEWZ

Copy this code and then press Enter to start the authentication process
(https://microsoft.com/devicelogin) (Press 'Enter' to confirm or 'Escape' to cancel)

FIGURE 5-18

Some text is automatically generated and displayed in the pane. Copy the text (because you're going to need it shortly) and press Enter. A browser will open, and you will be asked to authenticate against Azure DevOps. Once you have logged in, the web page will prompt you for the code that you just copied. Provide the code and click OK. The result, after these steps, is that you have now authenticated Visual Studio Code with Azure DevOps through your credentials, and the repository is ready to be used.

SUMMARY

All projects of any significant size will be using source control in some form or another, and good arguments can be made that even small projects should use source control. The result is that having built-in functionality that can be used by a wide variety of source control managers is very beneficial to developers.

In this chapter, we looked at the SCM provider that is included with Visual Studio Code (that is, Git) as well as how to integrate extensions that allow other SCM providers to be used. But most important for developers, the flow of checking out, changing, and checking back in is consistent across the different providers and is easy to do without needing to utilize additional tools on your machine.

Debugging Code

WHAT'S IN THIS CHAPTER?

➤ Understanding how to launch applications from within Visual Studio Code

➤ Learning about the various debug actions that are supported

➤ Creating launch configurations that support multiple simultaneous debug sessions

By now, it has been pretty well established that Visual Studio Code is a solid editor. And perhaps even a little better than solid. But if you're coming from a more "full-featured" development environment (thinking of you, Visual Studio and Eclipse), having an extraordinary editor isn't enough. You're used to being able to execute and debug your application from within your IDE. And while you can use other tools to debug web applications, it's still really convenient to have editing, executing, and debugging in one place.

Fortunately, Visual Studio Code can meet this requirement. In this chapter, we look at how to debug your web application from within the IDE. Although a number of debugger extensions allow other languages to be debugged, the capabilities that are native to Visual Studio Code are impressive.

DEBUGGING NODE.JS

Being able to use your editor as a debugging environment is a powerful idea. This is even more true when you're working in a web environment, where the web server frequently detects changes in the files and reloads all or part of the application dynamically.

Visual Studio Code comes with the ability to debug Node.js applications without additional installations required. This section will walk through the debugging experience using a sample application available when you first install Node.js.

Before you can debug Node.js, you need to install it. You can find instructions to install Node.js and a walkthrough that creates the sample application we'll use at `https://code.visualstudio.com/docs/nodejs/nodejs-tutorial`.

Launching the Session

In the simplest of cases, you can launch the debugger for Visual Studio Code against the currently open file. That would work just fine for the one-file sample app that was created in the tutorial. However, for real-world applications (not to mention many sample apps), that's not sufficient.

But there are still things to be learned by working through the simple case, so let's start by running the sample app through the debugger. Start by opening the Debug pane, either by using the Debug icon in the Activity Bar, or by using the View ➪ Debug menu item. The pane shown in Figure 6-1 appears.

With no previously defined configuration, running the application (by clicking the green triangle to the left of the Configuration drop-down) will launch the currently edited file. The Debug Console is opened and, assuming that the app.js file from the sample app is open, the results are shown in Figure 6-2.

The Debug Console has been opened and the output from the debugging session is displayed. It contains the node command that was executed to start the application, the message informing you that a debugger listener was attached to a local web socket URL (the `ws://` protocol indicates that it's a web socket), and the output from the application.

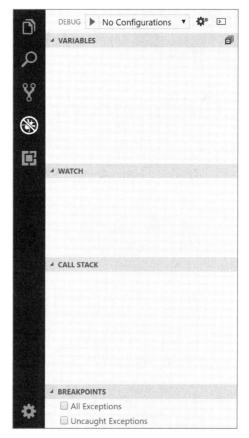

FIGURE 6-1

It's natural to wonder where, in the absence of any configuration, all of this activity came from. It has to do with how Visual Studio Code perceives the JavaScript file. From its perspective, JavaScript files are executed using Node.js. There is a default configuration for debugging Node.js applications that involves starting Node.js and attaching a listener for any debug output from the application.

Though this is the simple case, it's not exceptionally realistic; this is another way of suggesting that as your application gets more complicated than "Hello world," your debugging setup will become more complex, too. So let's look at some more realistic scenarios.

FIGURE 6-2

Launch Configurations

Since launching the current file isn't what real applications do, Visual Studio Code includes a `launch.json` file to provide more specific configuration for debugging.

> **NOTE** *The* `launch.json` *file is placed into the* .vscode *directory. And in order for debugging to work in Visual Studio Code, you have to have opened a folder. In other words, if you open a single file for editing, you can't execute and debug that file. There is no associated* .vscode *directory while editing a single file, and therefore no* `launch.json` *file to find.*

The contents of the `launch.json` file are actually up to the debugger. You might be surprised at the reference to a debugger as a separate entity. If you're familiar with development environments like Visual Studio or Eclipse, the debugger is just part of the application. But that's not the case with Visual Studio Code. Here, debugging is a language-based feature; that is, the debugger for JavaScript is not the same as the debugger for C#. Each language has its own. This approach has a number of benefits, an important one being extensibility to different languages. Just as IntelliSense support for different languages can be added through extensions, so, too, can debugger support.

While the specific contents of `launch.json` are up to the debugger, a couple of constraints do exist. It has to be a JSON-formatted file, and the following attributes must be present:

➤   `type`—Indicates the type of debugger that will process the JSON file.

➤ `request`—The type of debugging associated with this configuration. The valid choices are `launch` and `attach`, used when you launch a process or attach to a running process, respectively.

➤ `name`—The friendly name for the configuration.

Clicking the gear icon to the right of the configuration drop-down shown in Figure 6-1 automatically creates the launch.json file. Figure 6-3 shows what it looks like.

```
{} launch.json  ✕

    // Use IntelliSense to learn about possible attributes.
    // Hover to view descriptions of existing attributes.
    // For more information, visit: https://go.microsoft.com/fwlink/?link
    "version": "0.2.0",
    "configurations": [
        {
            "type": "node",
            "request": "launch",
            "name": "Launch Program",
            "program": "${workspaceFolder}\\app.js"
        }
    ]
}
```

Add Configuration...

FIGURE 6-3

You can see that the three basic attributes described earlier have been given values of `node`, `launch`, and `Launch Program`. Change the `name` attribute to **VSCode Sample Launch**. You'll also notice that there is an attribute named `program`. This is the path to the file that will be executed when the debugger launches. It has been defaulted to the currently edited file. It also uses variable substitution to indicate the current workspace directory. Variable substitutions are covered in their own section later in this chapter.

If you look at the File Explorer (shown in Figure 6-4), you'll see that a `.vscode` directory has been created and the launch.json file has been added to it.

In the editor for `launch.json`, you'll notice a large button labeled Add Configuration toward the bottom right. The purpose of this button is covered in the "Adding a Configuration" section later in this chapter.

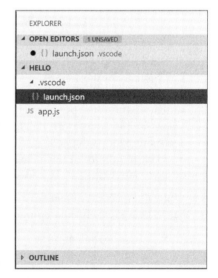

FIGURE 6-4

While only the three attributes are required, there is a collection of attributes commonly found in debuggers. After all, the main purpose of a debugger doesn't change significantly as you move from language to language. In this instance, IntelliSense is an invaluable development companion. In any `launch.json` file, using the Ctrl+Space command should display the range of attributes. If you have used an attribute that is not recognized by the target, IntelliSense will underline that attribute with a green squiggle. So, especially in `launch.json`, don't ignore what IntelliSense is telling you about the validity of the content.

To give you a sense of the kind of functionality that `launch.json` can support, here is a list of attributes that are frequently supported by different debuggers.

- ➤ `program`—Specifies the file (be it executable or script) that is run when the debugger is launched.

- ➤ `args`—The list of any arguments that are passed to the program when it is launched.

- ➤ `env`—The environment variables that are associated with the debug session.

- ➤ `cwd`—The current working directory, used within the debug session to identify the anchor for any relative paths.

- ➤ `port`—The port number to use when the debugger is attaching to the running process.

- ➤ `console`—The type of console to use. The most common options are the internal console (shown in Figure 6-2), the internal terminal (the terminal pane within Visual Studio Code), and the external terminal (an external window associated with the debugger).

- ➤ `serverReadyAction`—Used to automatically open a URL in a web browser at an appropriate point in the debugging session. The details of this attribute are covered later in this chapter.

- ➤ `preLaunchTask`—Identifies a task that should be launched prior to initiating the debug session.

- ➤ `postDebugTask`—Identifies a task that should be launched as the final step in the debug session.

A quick note about those last two attributes. While naturally the specifics about how to identify and execute the task will depend on the debugger, in many cases, a common format is used. Visual Studio Code supports a `tasks.json` file (found in the `.vscode` folder) that contains task information. You can find more details about the structure and usage of the `tasks.json` in Chapter 7, "External Tools and Task Automation."

Launch vs. Attach Execution

Depending on your development experience, you might look at the idea of launching an application in order to test it a little odd. If you are a frontend developer, for instance, your browser is probably constantly open. You make changes to the underlying files and your application reloads automatically. Certainly, you don't need to relaunch your browser. If you need to debug your JavaScript, you use the developer tools that are included in the browser. Those tools are actually "attached" to the current instance of your browser in order to view and manipulate what's happening during execution.

On the other hand, consider a backend developer. Backend developers are more familiar with launching the server with a debugger automatically attached. They put breakpoints into their code and when requests come in, they can stop the execution, see what's going on, and then return the results to the requester. The debugger still needs to be attached to the server, but that happens automatically when the server is launched without requiring a separate action.

As you can see, these are markedly different experiences, and they require different processes related to debugging. For this reason, Visual Studio Code supports both the concept of a launch configuration and an attach configuration.

The easiest way to visualize the difference is to consider a launch configuration as describing how to start a process and then attaching a debugger to it. An attach configuration describes how to attach the debugger to an existing process. In case you were wondering why `program` is not a required attribute for `launch.json`, it's because in the case of an attach configuration, it's not necessary. You're not running a program; instead, you're attaching to a port through which debugging activity occurs.

Adding a Configuration

It is possible to have multiple configurations defined within the `launch.json` file. Then, as you start the application, you can choose which configuration you use. This allows you to attach to an existing process or launch a new process from the same workspace, depending on your choice. Or you can have different starting programs, or tasks, or different parameters, all based on the configuration you choose.

The process of adding a configuration is straightforward. As mentioned earlier, when editing the `launch.json` file, there is a large button labeled Add Configuration in the bottom-right corner of the editor. To add a new configuration, click the button. This launches the code snippet process for the `launch.json` file, as shown in Figure 6-5.

As you can see, a number of options are available. The Attach, Attach To Process, and Attach To Remote Program options create configurations that are used to attach to running applications. The Launch Program and Launch Via NPM options are used to launch a specific program or to use NPM to run a script. The differences between these options are as follows:

➤ *Attach*—Attaches to a running process by connecting to a specific port. The presumption is that the process is already running and will communicate with the debugger on that port.

➤ *Attach To Process*—Attaches to a running process that is identified by process ID. When this debug session is launched, you will be prompted to select the process to which you want to attach.

➤ *Attach To Remote Program*—Attaches to a program running on a remote machine.

➤ *Launch A Program*—Launches a specific program.

➤ *Launch Via NPM*—Starts running the Node.js Package Manager (NPM) process, then executes a script as specified by the arguments to the command.

FIGURE 6-5

Once you have defined multiple configurations, the next step is to specify the configuration you want to use at runtime. Back in the Debug pane, shown in Figure 6-6, there is an option just for this purpose.

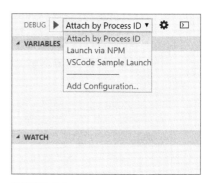

The drop-down list at the top of the pane contains a list of the configurations defined in `launch.json`. More precisely, it contains the `name` attribute for each of the configurations (the reason why the `name` attribute was required). Choose the desired configuration from the drop-down and click the Run button to launch (or attach) using that configuration. If you start the debug session using the Debug ⇨ Start Debugging menu option, it uses the currently selected configuration. Once you have selected a configuration, the active configuration appears in the Status Bar at the bottom of the IDE (see Figure 6-7).

FIGURE 6-6

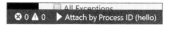

FIGURE 6-7

Not only does the configuration appear in the Status Bar, but you can also start the debugging session through the Status Bar. Clicking the configuration in the Status Bar, as is visible in Figure 6-7, starts the debugging process.

Simultaneous Configurations

Depending on the complexity of your application, there might be times when you need to run multiple processes as part of a single debugging session. A possible scenario that requires this is if your server code is executed separately from your client code. Fortunately, Visual Studio Code supports the ability to run multiple configurations simultaneously, and will attach a debugger to each process, giving you an end-to-end-and-back-again debugging experience.

You have two ways to run multiple debugging sessions simultaneously. The first is ad hoc. Start by launching one session. Then, once it has started, launch a second session. At this point, Visual Studio Code goes into *multi-target mode*.

Before going into the details of multi-target mode, let's consider the second method for running multiple debugging sessions, as this technique is much less ad hoc.

To start, open up the `launch.json` file. Then add an attribute at the top level that looks like the following:

```json
"compounds": [
  {
    "name": "Console/Node",
    "configurations": [
      ".NET Core Launch (console)",
      "VSCode Sample Launch"
    ]
  }
]
```

The `compounds` attribute defines a compound configuration (named Console/Node) that combines the .NET Core Launch (console) configuration with the VSCode Sample Launch configuration. This configuration now appears in the drop-down that was shown in Figure 6-6, so you can choose it when you launch your debugging session.

When Visual Studio Code goes into multi-target mode, a couple of things change slightly. First, every debugging session has a debug toolbar. An example of the toolbar is shown in Figure 6-8.

FIGURE 6-8

While the details of this toolbar are covered in the next section, "Debug Actions," notice the drop-down on the right side. This list contains the currently running sessions. By choosing a particular session, you direct the debug actions that are triggered by the buttons on the toolbar to the appropriate session.

The second change is in the Call Stack section of the Debug pane (Figure 6-9).

You can see two nodes in the figure, one for each of the debugging sessions. Below each node is the current call stack for the node. This allows you to interact with each session independently while still seeing all of the relevant information in one place.

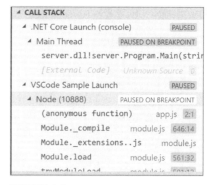

FIGURE 6-9

Debug Actions

Now that you have learned how to go about starting a debugging session, let's consider the functionality that's available while you're debugging. As a starting point, let's begin with the basic functionality of breakpoints.

Breakpoints

A breakpoint is used to pause an application at a particular point of execution. An application that has been paused is in Break mode, causing many of the debug actions to become active. You can set breakpoints either through the editor or by using a keyboard shortcut (which is F9 by default). The simplest way is to click the left margin in the editor. A red dot appears, indicating that a breakpoint has been set (see Figure 6-10).

FIGURE 6-10

Clicking a second time clears the breakpoint. If you're using the keyboard shortcut to set or clear breakpoints, it operates on the current line, toggling the breakpoint as needed.

Once a breakpoint has been specified for a line, additional details for the breakpoint can be specified through the right-click context menu (shown in Figure 6-11).

Here you have options to remove the breakpoint completely or just disable the breakpoint. A disabled breakpoint will not pause execution if it is hit, but all of the settings for the breakpoint remain intact.

FIGURE 6-11

The third option in the context menu, Edit Breakpoint, is used to allow for more advanced breakpoint configuration. If you have used breakpoints in the past, you'll be familiar with needing to use the Continue command multiple times at the same breakpoint until the condition you're looking for is met. By using the Edit Breakpoint option, you open a small pane (Figure 6-12) that is used to create conditional breakpoints, thus minimizing this need for continuing.

FIGURE 6-12

Visual Studio Code supports two different types of conditions for breakpoints. The first, which is selected by choosing Expression from the drop-down, lets you compose an expression that is evaluated whenever the line is hit. If the expression evaluates to True, execution pauses at the breakpoint. Otherwise, execution continues. The expression can be any valid expression for the language in which the breakpoint is set. The only requirement is that it needs to evaluate to a Boolean.

The second type of condition is a hit count. The expression provided is the number of times the line must be executed before execution will be paused. The requirement here is that the expression must evaluate to an integer.

There is a third option in the drop-down for editing breakpoints, but it's not a different kind of condition. Instead, it's called a Logpoint, and it's defined by selecting Log Message from the drop-down. There is still an expression that needs to be provided, but instead of pausing execution, when the line of code is hit, the expression is evaluated and the result is sent to the Debug Console (or any other terminal set up as the target for debug output). This type of breakpoint can help identify issues in cases where stopping execution at a breakpoint actually prevents the issue from occurring.

Be aware that not every debugger supports conditional breakpoints or Logpoints. If that's the case, the Edit Breakpoint context menu item will be disabled.

Two other types of breakpoints might be supported by the debugger.

An Inline Breakpoint is a breakpoint that is triggered when execution reaches a particular column within the source code. It is useful if you're attempting to debug a minified file and the individual method calls aren't on separate lines. You can open up the file in question, right-click at the column where you'd like the breakpoint to be placed, and select Add Inline Breakpoint from the context menu. A breakpoint is created, and the red dot appears, both in the margin and at the point of the breakpoint. Figure 6-13 illustrates what this looks like.

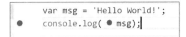

FIGURE 6-13

A Function Breakpoint is one where the name of the method is what triggers the pause in the execution. It would most likely be used when you're working with third-party code and, while you know the name of the method being called, you don't know (or have access to) where that method is implemented.

You create a Function Breakpoint by going through the Breakpoints panel in the Debug view (Figure 6-14).

FIGURE 6-14

The panel contains a list of all the breakpoints defined within the application. You can enable and disable individual breakpoints using the checkbox to the left of each breakpoint. In Figure 6-14, there is a breakpoint in the app.js file at line 2 (the line is the number at the extreme right). In addition, you can specify that execution is paused either on all exceptions or only on exceptions that are uncaught within the application.

To create a Function Breakpoint, click the plus sign in the title for the panel. This causes a text box to open in the list of breakpoints (seen in Figure 6-15).

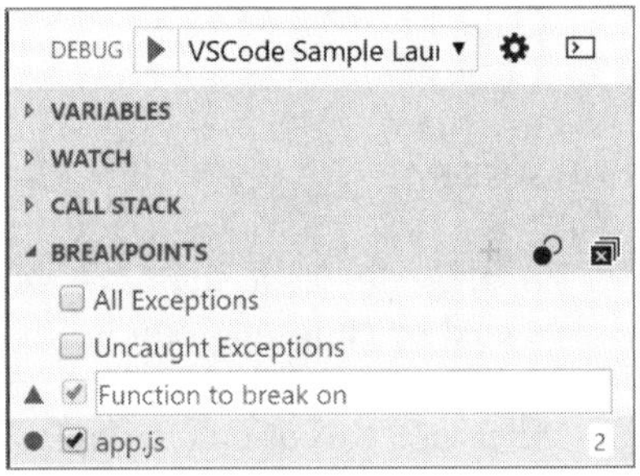

Now you can type in the name of the method and, if that method is ever hit, execution will be paused. Notice that instead of a red circle, a diamond is used for the Function Breakpoints.

FIGURE 6-15

Stepping through Code

Once you have paused the execution of your application, you have a number of options available to move execution forward. The choices are:

➤ *Step Over*—The line that currently has focus is executed and the execution point is set to the next line in the current code block. If the end of the code block has been reached, Step Over returns to the calling code block.

➤ *Step Into*—When on a simple statement such as a numeric operation or a cast, Step Into behaves the same as Step Over. When the line is more complex, Step Into steps through all user code. For example, if the current statement includes a method, Step Into will move the execution point to the first executable line in that method.

➤ *Step Out*—Step Out moves the execution point out of the current method and back to where the method was called. This is quite convenient if you are in the middle of a long method and you don't want to either step over every line in that method or set a breakpoint at the end of the method.

You can execute any one of these functions through a few user-interface options. First, as was shown in Figure 6-8, while in Debug mode, a toolbar is visible. Figure 6-16 shows the toolbar when you're not in multi-target mode.

FIGURE 6-16

The debug actions in the preceding list, along with a couple more, can be triggered through the toolbar. Specifically, the second icon (the arrow hopping over the dot) invokes the Step Over command. The third icon (downward arrow) invokes the Step Into command. The fourth icon (upward arrow) invokes Step Out.

Three other commands are also available in the toolbar. The first icon (the right-pointing triangle) is used to continue execution. Your application will continue executing and the debug actions won't become active unless and until execution is paused again.

The fifth icon (the circular arrow) is used to restart the application. In this case, execution is halted and a brand new debugging session is started. Finally, the last icon (the square) is used to terminate the current debugging session.

Data Inspection

While you are debugging your application, it's useful to be able to check on the value of variables that are being used. Within Visual Studio Code, you have two options for inspecting data at runtime.

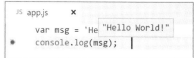

FIGURE 6-17

First, and probably the most convenient, is to hover your mouse over the variable you want to inspect. When you do this, the current value of the variable appears as a tooltip (an example is shown in Figure 6-17).

If you're coming from the Visual Studio world, you might be disappointed that you can't modify the variable's value through the tooltip. But the next location for viewing variables gives a way to accomplish that.

The second place where variable values can be seen is in the Variable panel in the Debug pane. Figure 6-18 illustrates the variables at the active breakpoint.

Here you can see both local variables (those defined within the scope of the current method) and global variables (which have values across more than one method). If the value is an object, the variable can be expanded using the triangle to the left of the name. In Figure 6-18, the module variable has been expanded so that the properties are visible.

Note that the variables and values shown in the local sections are context-dependent. The context, in this case, is the current process. If you are in multi-target mode, you can change the debugging context, and therefore the context for the variables, by clicking a different portion of the Call Stack section.

If you double-click the value for a particular property, you are given the chance to edit its value. Figure 6-19 shows what this looks like.

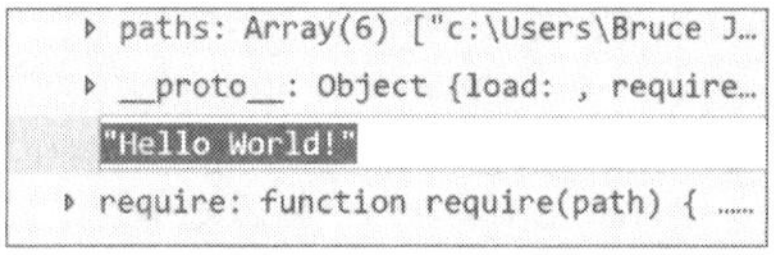

You can see that the msg variable has been replaced with a text box that contains the value. Make any changes you like (within reason) and hit the Enter key. This will cause the value to be modified throughout the rest of the application.

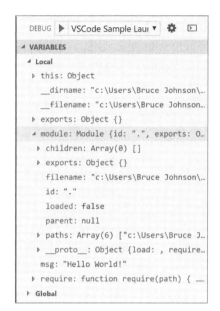

FIGURE 6-18

FIGURE 6-19

Advanced Launch Configuration

Earlier in the chapter, the basics of the launch.json file were examined. However, some advanced features are available that, while you might never use them, are handy tools to have in your toolbox. If you ever do need them, you'll be thrilled to know that they are part of Visual Studio Code.

Variable Substitution

If you go back to the beginning of the chapter and look at the launch.json file, you'll notice a number of places where non-specific values were used. Instead, placeholders were used that are intended to be given values only when the debugging session is begun. This functionality is known as *variable substitution* and, while its existence is dependent on the specific debugger, it's supported out of the box for Node.js debugging.

Variable substitution is supported for more than just launch.json. It is also used in the task.json file. You can find a complete description of the supported functionality in the "Variable Substitution" section of Chapter 7.

Launching a Browser on Debug

A frequent requirement is to have a browser launch when you start a debug session. However, it's not as simple as launching the browser and giving it a URL. What if the server (presuming that the server is part of the application that you're running) isn't ready when the browser starts up? Wouldn't it be better if the browser didn't launch until the server was ready? Of course it would.

Earlier in this chapter, we described the `serverReadyAction` attribute in the `launch.json` file. It becomes intrinsic to this functionality. To demonstrate, let's create a simple Hello World server application.

In Visual Studio Code, create a new file at the top level (the same level as the `app.js` file), and call the file **helloServer.js**. Then add the following code to the file:

```
var express = require('express');
var app = express();

app.get('/', function (req, res) {
  res.send('Hello World!')
});

app.listen(3000, function () {
  console.log('HelloServer listening on port 3000!')
});
```

The server functionality depends on the Node.js Express component, so it needs to be added to the project. To do this, open the Terminal (using the View ⇨ Terminal menu option) and execute the command **npm install express**.

Now that the application is ready to run, let's look at the `launch.json` file. To start with, we'll add a configuration that will run this server. Add the following to the existing `launch.json` file as the last element in the `configurations array` attribute:

```
{
    "type": "node",
    "request": "launch",
    "name": "Sample Server",
    "program": "${workspaceFolder}\\helloServer.js",
}
```

In the Debug pane, select the Sample Server configuration and run the application. The Debug Console should look something similar to Figure 6-20.

```
PROBLEMS    OUTPUT    DEBUG CONSOLE    TERMINAL                          ⅺ  ∧  ✕

 C:\Program Files\nodejs\node.exe --inspect-brk=16921 helloServer.js
 Debugger listening on ws://127.0.0.1:16921/10e2d7da-6eb4-48c3-a7a0-5f18a630bd84
 HelloServer listening on port 3000!                              helloServer.js:9
```

FIGURE 6-20

Notice that when the server starts, a message in the Debug Console says `HelloServer listening on port 3000!`. That is the message that we want the `serverReadyAction` to detect. So stop running the application and go back into the `launch.json` file. Add the following attribute to the configuration you just added:

```
"serverReadyAction": {
    "pattern": "listening on port ([0-9]+)",
    "uriFormat": "http://localhost:%s",
    "action": "openExternally"
}
```

The `pattern` attribute value is a regular expression that is compared to the messages displayed in the Debug Console. In this case, it's looking for the string `listening on port nnnn` and it will extract the numeric value after `port`. The `uriFormat` attribute is an expression that gets evaluated to produce the URL for the browser. Finally, the `action` attribute says to open the URL using an external application (which, in this case, will be your default browser). When you run the application, the browser is displayed with the "Hello World!" message visible (see Figure 6-21).

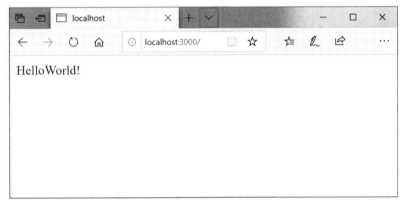

FIGURE 6-21

SUMMARY

The ability to debug your applications through Visual Studio Code is a powerful feature. The information that's available at your fingertips, and the flexibility in terms of launching options, are compelling reasons to use Visual Studio Code for the entire development workflow.

Ultimately, it's possible to have an end-to-end launching and debugging experience. If you develop web applications, whether you're a client-side developer, a backend specialist, or both, it's hard to ignore how much easier (and more fun) it is to track down bugs.

7

External Tools and Task Automation

WHAT'S IN THIS CHAPTER?

➤   Understanding how to execute tasks from within Visual Studio Code

➤   Learning about the capabilities of Visual Studio Code when it comes to custom tasks

➤   Working with problem matchers and variable substitution to create generic tasks

The development of modern web applications is not just a matter of writing some JavaScript, or Python, or PHP, or any other single language. Today's code lives within an ecosystem of tools that perform various functions, from ensuring code quality to producing efficient packages for deployment.

And this isn't just limited to web applications. Regardless of the language being used and the platform being targeted, some tasks are routinely performed as part of the development and testing workflow.

To be able to truly fit into how today's developers work, Visual Studio Code has to be able to work seamlessly with these tools—and it does. In this chapter, we'll look at how you can use linters, transpilers, minifiers, and the like within your regular workflow.

TASKS DEFINED

The connection between Visual Studio Code and external tools is through a collection of defined tasks. For most tools, their preferred method of execution is through a command-line interface. So, at the heart of a task is the ability to execute a command line, then capture and process the results. And, of course, to do this in a generic manner that can be applied to many different tools.

As a starting point, let's go through the process of creating a simple (and relatively common) task. For this example, we're going to process a TypeScript file (the process is typically called *compiling* or, more precisely, *transpiling*) into JavaScript.

For the example task, open up your favorite command-line window and execute the following commands:

```
mkdir sample-task
cd sample-task
tsc --init
code .
```

The `tsc` command with the `init` option is used to create the `tsconfig.json` file. To transpile TypeScript, you need to have the `typescript` package available. If you had previously installed TypeScript on your system, there shouldn't be any issues. But if you execute the `tsc` command and the command is not found, try running the command **npm install -g typescript** to load the package into your project.

Once Visual Studio Code is running, create a file called `greeting.ts`. The contents of this newly created file are as follows:

```
function greeting(name: string): void {
    console.log('Hello ${name}!');
}

greeting('Snickers');
```

Now that the example is ready to go, let's check out the tasks that are available. Execute the Terminal ⇨ Run Build Task menu command. This displays the pane shown in Figure 7-1.

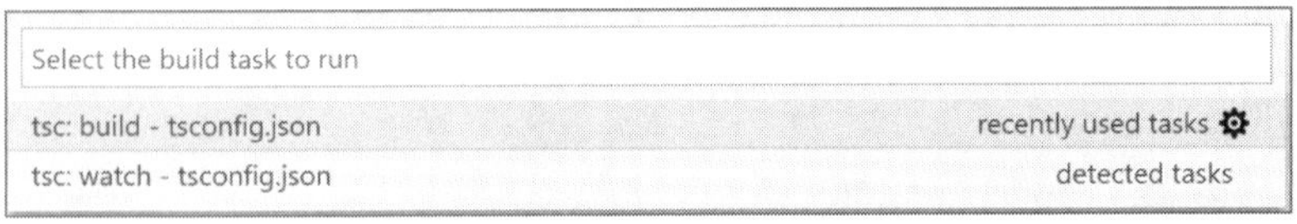

FIGURE 7-1

As a result of the presence of the `tsconfig.json` file, Visual Studio Code has automatically detected and exposed two commands. These two tasks are provided by the TypeScript language service. The `tsc: build` command performs a build on your workspace. The `tsc: watch` command starts the compiler in watch mode. That way, if there are changes to your files, they are automatically compiled. You can execute either of these tasks by clicking the item in the list.

You might find it annoying that every time you want to build or watch your TypeScript files, you have to execute the Run Build Task command and then select from a list of options. It's propitious that the Visual Studio Code team felt the same way. As a result, it's possible to define one of the tasks as being the default.

In the Terminal menu, select the Configure Default Build Task option. This displays the same pane shown in Figure 7-1. However, once you choose a task, a `tasks.json` file is created (and placed into the `.vscode` folder) where the selected task is defined as being the default. The following is the `tasks.json` file generated when the watch task is selected as the default:

```json
{
    "version": "2.0.0",
    "tasks": [
        {
            "type": "typescript",
            "tsconfig": "tsconfig.json",
            "option": "watch",
            "problemMatcher": [
                "$tsc-watch"
            ],
            "group": {
                "kind": "build",
                "isDefault": true
            }
        }
    ]
}
```

The attribute that makes this task the default is the `isDefault` attribute in the `group` property. The `kind` attribute is what indicates that the task is a build task. That means it will appear in the list associated with the Run Build Tasks command. Otherwise, it will just be available in the Run Tasks command.

Visual Studio Code automatically detects tasks for a number of different systems: Grunt, Gulp, Jake, and Node Package Manager (npm). What this means is that they don't appear in a `tasks.json` file. Instead, they are defined in the configuration file for each of those task runners. However, Visual Studio Code knows the format of those files, so they are available when you execute the Run Tasks command. For the most part, this is an incredibly convenient feature. It keeps developers from having to configure the `tasks.json` file for a set of tasks defined in a different config file. And anything that reduces configuration, not to mention the challenge of keeping the two files in sync, is an increase in productivity.

But for those situations that don't fit neatly into the automatically detected tasks, Visual Studio Code does provide a couple of escape hatches. First, you can modify the settings so that automatic detection is not performed for each of the systems. The following JSON illustrates the settings when each of them has been turned off:

```json
{
    "grunt.autoDetect": "off",
    "gulp.autoDetect": "off",
    "jake.autoDetect": "off",
    "npm.autoDetect": "off"
    "typescript.tsc.autoDetect": "off",
}
```

It's more likely that disabling automatic detection is the scenario where you want to modify the detected tasks in some manner. To get to the point where this is possible, you need to add the necessary configuration to the `tasks.json` file. If you look back at Figure 7-1, you'll notice a gear on the far right of the task. This gear appears when your mouse hovers over a task. Clicking that gear adds the configuration for that task to the `tasks.json` file. Now you can customize it as you want. A description of how to customize the configuration (or to create tasks of your own) is covered in the next section.

CREATING CUSTOM TASKS

As nice as it is for tasks to be automatically detected, in some instances that is not sufficient for the task (pun intended) at hand. For instance, before running a suite of tests, you might want to execute a script that sets up and initializes the test environment. Visual Studio Code is not limited to just the built-in tasks. In this section, we take a look at the options available for you to create your own tasks.

The starting point is to create a `tasks.json` file, if your workspace doesn't have one already. If you have worked through the examples earlier in this chapter, you already have one that you can work with. If not, use the Terminal ➪ Configure Tasks option to display the pane shown in Figure 7-2.

Select a task to configure
tsc: build - tsconfig.json
tsc: watch - tsconfig.json
Create tasks.json file from template

FIGURE 7-2

You'll notice that, along with the auto-detected tasks, there is an option to create the `tasks.json` from a template. Choose that option and the pane shown in Figure 7-3 appears.

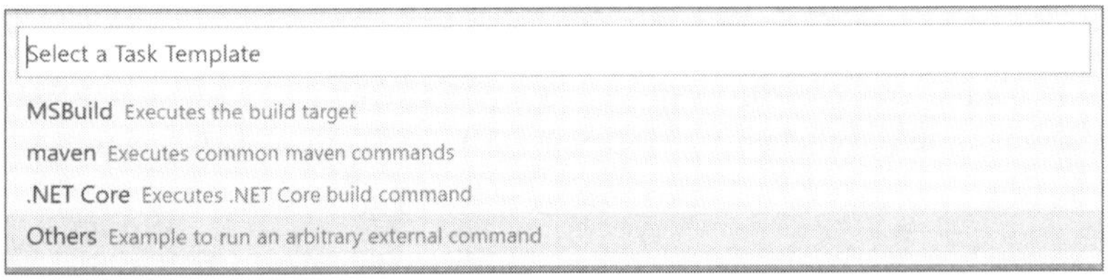

Select a Task Template
MSBuild Executes the build target
maven Executes common maven commands
.NET Core Executes .NET Core build command
Others Example to run an arbitrary external command

FIGURE 7-3

The list in Figure 7-3 contains the task runners that are available on your machine. If you install a different task runner (like grunt or gulp), you'll see that name appear in the list.

> **NOTE** *A task runner is pretty much exactly what the name says: it's a tool that is used to run tasks. The goal is to automate the commands that a developer might otherwise have to do manually. This is even more important when a task needs to be executed frequently, such as the transpiling of TypeScript or the minification of JavaScript files.*

Each of them has a different template for use in the `tasks.json` file, but for this example, select Others to use the generic template. A `tasks.json` file is created with the following contents:

```
{
    "version": "2.0.0",
    "tasks": [
        {
            "label": "echo",
            "type": "shell",
            "command": "echo Hello"
        }
    ]
}
```

The `tasks` attribute is actually an array where each element in the array is a JSON object representing a task. The generic task only has three attributes:

➤ `label`—A user-friendly name for the tasks, used when lists of tasks get displayed.

➤ `type`—The type of task. For a custom task (that is, one not being executed by a task provider that is part of an extension), the only options are `shell` and `process`. For a type of `shell`, the command is interpreted as a shell command. For a type of `process`, the command is interpreted as an executable to be launched.

➤ `command`—The actual command that is to be executed.

As you might expect, these are not the only options that are available. While the following list is not complete, it does cover a lot of the scenarios that would be considered typical:

➤ `group`—Used to define the group into which this task falls. Two groups within Visual Studio Code are important: `build` and `test`. All the tasks that are part of the `build` group appear when you use the Run Build Task command. And, not coincidentally, the tasks that are part of the `test` group appear when you use the Run Test Task command.

The `group` attribute can be a little more complex than simply the name of the group. It can actually be a JSON object in itself. Following is a snippet where it is more completely defined:

```
"group": {
    "kind": "build",
    "isDefault": true
}
```

What used to be the group name (that is, `build` or `test`) is now the `kind` attribute. And there is a second attribute, `isDefault`, which indicates that the task is the default for that kind.

➤ `presentation`—Determines how the output from the task is displayed in Visual Studio Code.

The value for this attribute is a JSON object with four attributes.

➤ `echo`—A Boolean that determines if the command associated with the task is displayed in the user interface.

➤ `focus`—A Boolean that determines if the panel showing the task output will be given focus.

➤ panel—Specifies which instance of a panel will be used for the task. The options are: shared (the panel will be shared between multiple tasks), dedicated (a panel will be created that gets output from this task every time it runs), or new (a new panel is created with each task execution).

➤ reveal—Determines if the task's output is displayed in the user interface. The choices are never, silent, and always. The values of never and always means to never show output or always show output, respectively. The silent option shows the output but doesn't allow any user input to be requested.

Two additional attributes are covered elsewhere in this chapter: the problemMatcher attribute, which determines how the output from the task is interpreted, and the options attribute, which allows for differences between the platforms to be addressed. These are covered in the "Problem Matchers" and "Platform-Specific Properties" sections, later in this chapter.

Compound Tasks

As you might have surmised, given that the tasks attribute in tasks.json is an array, it's possible to have more than one task defined. All of the tasks are available to execute through one of the options in the Terminal menu (Run Tasks, Run Build Tasks, Run Test Tasks).

However, it is likely that, at least some of the time, multiple tasks should be run as a unit, or that the tasks are related in that one should be run prior to another. The dependsOn attribute provides this functionality.

You have two ways to utilize dependsOn. Consider the following task definitions:

```
{
    "version": "2.0.0",
    "tasks": [
        {
            "label": "Step One",
            "type": "shell",
            "command": "echo Step 1"
        },
        {
            "label": "Step Two",
            "type": "shell",
            "command": "echo Step 2"
        }
    ]
}
```

First, you can create a dependency between Step Two and Step One such that Step One needs to be executed first. You do this by adding a dependsOn attribute to the Step Two definition as follows:

```
{
    "label": "Step Two",
    "type": "shell",
    "command": "echo Step 2",
    "dependsOn": ["Step One"]
}
```

You can also create a new task that comprises the two existing tasks with the task definition shown here:

```
{
    "label": "Compound Task",
    "dependsOn": ["Step One", "Step Two"]
}
```

The one thing to be aware of when you chain tasks together like this is that the tasks will run in parallel. So, if there is a dependency between the tasks (like the build needs to run before a minifier), you can't simply include both tasks in the list.

PROBLEM MATCHERS

If you think about the job of task processing within Visual Studio Code, you'll realize that there is a challenge in finding generic ways of getting status information pushed back into Visual Studio Code. For instance, if there is a syntax problem with your code, a message appears in the Problems tab. It would be handy if the output from a task, especially if issues exist, could appear in the same tab.

The problem matcher concept is designed to address this situation. A problem matcher is specific to the command being executed in a task. It understands the output (or, more precisely, the format of the output) so that it knows when errors or warnings have occurred and transfers that information to the Problems tab.

Visual Studio Code has a number of built-in problem matchers. These are designed to cover many of the common tools that are used within the IDE, including C#, ESLint, Go, JSHint, Less, Sass, TypeScript, and Visual Basic.

While that's a decent list, in some cases you'll need to create your own problem matcher. You can do this by using regular expression matching on the output from the task. As a result, the definition of the problem matcher needs to be associated with the task, and there is a `problemMatcher` attribute that does just that. Here is an example `problemMatcher`:

```
"problemMatcher": {
    "owner": "cpp",
    "fileLocation": ["relative", "${workspaceFolder}"],
    "pattern": {
        "regexp": "^(.*):(\\d+):(\\d+):\\s+(warning|error):\\s+(.*)$",
        "file": 1,
        "line": 2,
        "column": 3,
        "severity": 4,
        "message": 5
    }
}
```

The components of the problem matcher are actually surprisingly straightforward:

➤ owner—The name of the language service that owns the problem matcher. This is used to restrict when the problem matcher needs to be used.

➤ `fileLocation`—The location of the file that is related to the errors. In the example, any file-name that appears in the output is relative to the `workspaceFolder`. The idea is to be able to locate the file if only the filename is in the output (as opposed to the full path).

➤ `pattern`—This is the meat of the pattern matcher. It is the regular expression against which each line in the output from the task will be processed. Notice that there are a number of captures in the expression. Those captures are used in the other attributes.

➤ `file`, `line`, `column`, `severity`, `message`—These property names map to the output that appears in the Problems tab. The value assigned to each one is the number of the capture from the regular expression that contains the file. For instance, if the second capture contains the filename, then the `file` attribute would be given a value of 2. It's not necessary to provide values for any of these properties. They are present only so that the information can used in the Problems list.

Multiline Matchers

There might be instances where the output from the task spans more than one line in the output file. Indeed, you could have output that looks like the following:

```
Filename.ext:
    Line 5: bad stuff happened
    Line 7: more bad stuff happened
```

To handle multiple lines in the output, you create an array of patterns:

```
"pattern": [
    {
        "regexp": "^([^\\s].*)$",
        "file": 1
    },
    {
        "regexp": "^Line (\\d+):\\s+(.*)$",
        "line": 2,
        "message": 3
    }
]
```

The first pattern in the array matches the first line, the one containing the name of the file. The second pattern matches the error message that is tied to a specific line. You'll notice that even though multiple patterns are being matched, each of the Problems tab properties would only appear once.

Of course, this pattern doesn't quite cover the described scenario. In the output file, there was a single line containing a file, but multiple lines for the errors. This is addressed by adding a `loop` attribute to the last pattern in the array. The final pattern is shown here:

```
"pattern": [
    {
        "regexp": "^([^\\s].*)$",
        "file": 1
    },
    {
        "regexp": "^Line (\\d+):\\s+(.*)$",
        "line": 2,
        "message": 3,
        "loop": true
    }
]
```

Background Patterns

A number of tools (like gulp or tsc) have tasks that support watching the file system and then, upon a change, will start execution. And, just like a regular task, you need to be able to process the output so that any errors can be displayed in the Problems pane. The difference is that you're likely to have output that looks like the following:

```
Change detected - Started processing
Filename.ext:
   Line 5: bad stuff happened
   Line 7: more bad stuff happened
Ready - Watching for file changes
```

The starting point for handling this is the task that was created in the last section. There is a `background` attribute for the task that needs to be set to true in order to trigger the background processing. This allows the task to run in the background and watch the output for the starting pattern. Once the starting pattern is discovered, all of the output is run through the usual regular expressions for the problem matching until the ending pattern is found. So for the preceding output, the task definition would be as follows:

```
{
    "version": "2.0.0",
    "tasks": [
        {
            "label": "background",
            "type": "shell",
            "command": "backgroundWatcher.cmd",
            "background": true,
            "problemMatcher": {
                "owner": "cpp",
                "fileLocation": ["relative", "${workspaceFolder}"],
                "pattern": [
                    {
                        "regexp": "^([^\\s].*)$",
                        "file": 1
                    },
                    {
                        "regexp": "^Line (\\d+):\\s+(.*)$",
                        "line": 2,
                        "message": 3,
                        "loop": true
                    }
                ],
                "background": {
                    "activeOnStart": true,
                    "beginsPattern": "^Change detected - Stared processing$",
                    "endsPattern": "^Ready - Watching for file changes
$"
                }
            }
        }
    ]
}
```

ADVANCED TASK CONFIGURATION

As much as the configuration of tasks might seem pretty thorough, a couple of cases still require additional attention.

Platform-Specific Properties

Both `tasks.json` and `launch.json` support defining values (for example, arguments to be passed to the program) that depend on the operating system where the debugger is running. To do so, put a platform-specific literal into the JSON file and specify the corresponding properties inside that literal.

Following is an example that executes a single task differently on Windows than on the other platforms:

```json
{
    "version": "2.0.0",
    "tasks": [
        {
            "label": "Run setup",
            "type": "shell",
            "command": ".\scripts\setup.sh",
            "windows": {
                "command": ".\\scripts\\setup.cmd"
            }
        }
    ]
}
```

Valid operating properties are `"windows"` for Windows, `"linux"` for Linux, and `"osx"` for macOS. Properties defined in an operating-system-specific scope override properties defined in the global scope.

Variable Substitution

If you think about the different arguments that could be passed into a particular task, it's not hard to imagine needing to provide context-related values, like the name of the program or the path to a particular file. We can all agree that hardcoding values is not the best way to go, at least not in the long term. Instead, it would be better to use placeholders that are intended to be given values only when the debugging session begins. This functionality is known as variable substitution and, while its existence is dependent on the specific debugger, it's supported out of the box for Node.js debugging.

The premise behind variable substation is not unique. At any point in the `launch.json` or `tasks.json` file, you can specify a placeholder. The placeholder takes the form of ${name}, where name is the identifier of the placeholder. Then, when a debugging session is started for that configuration, the placeholders are replaced with current values. The list of supported placeholder names is as follows:

➤ `cwd`—The current working directory for the task runner. The task runner is the process that is interpreting the JSON file and using it to start the debugging session.

➤ `execPath`—The path to the running executable for Visual Studio Code.

➤ `file`—The path to the currently opened file.

- ➤ fileBasename—The base name for the currently opened file.

- ➤ fileBasenameNoExtension—The base name of the currently open file, but without the file extension.

- ➤ fileDirname—The name of the directory for the currently open file.

- ➤ fileExtname—The extension for the currently open file.

- ➤ lineNumber—The line number for the line that is currently selected in the active file.

- ➤ relativeFile—The path to the currently open file, relative to workspaceFolder.

- ➤ selectedText—The currently selected text in the active file.

- ➤ workspaceFolder—The path of the currently open folder (that is, opened in Visual Studio Code).

- ➤ workspaceFolderBasename—The name of the currently open folder without any slashes.

You can also access environment variables within the JSON files. The pattern for the placeholder is ${env:name}, where name is the name of the environment variable.

Please know that case matters. Make sure that the name of the environment variable used in the placeholder matches the name in your platform.

The configuration values for Visual Studio Code can also be referenced within the file. The pattern is ${config:name}, where name is the full name of the configuration value.

Finally, if accessing variable values isn't sufficient, you can execute a command. The pattern is ${command:commandId}, where commandId is the identifier for the command.

The processing of the command is very dependent on the command itself. If executing the command simply returns a value, that value is substituted with no additional effort. However, the command might show a sophisticated user interface. In that case, the interface is displayed and the user will enter values and confirm their input before the processing continues.

One weakness in these substitutions is that you can't prompt the user for a value upon starting the debug session. This is addressed through the implementation of input variables. The pattern for an input variable is ${input:variableId}, where variableId is the identifier for the variable.

The variable identifier is an index into the inputs section of the JSON. You would create a section that looks like the following:

```
"inputs": [
    {
        "id": "variableID",
        "type": "type of input variable",
        ...
    },
    ...
]
```

Three different types of input variables impact the other attributes found in the input JSON object:

➤ `promptString`—This input type prompts the user for a value. There is a `description` attribute shown in the input box and a `default` attribute that defines the value in the absence of any user input.

➤ `pickString`—Prompts the user to select from a list of options. Like `promptString`, there is a `description` and a `default` attribute, but there is also an `options` attribute that contains an array of the values to be displayed in the list.

➤ `command`—Causes a specific command to be executed. There is a `command` attribute that contains the full name of the command to be executed, along with an `args` attribute that is a JSON object of properties to be used by the command.

SUMMARY

The development flow for modern applications has very much fallen into the edit, compile, test, debug loop. Since this loop is repeated over and over and over, any improvements that can be made to streamline the steps can greatly increase productivity.

Many command-line tools are available whose job it is to do just that. Those tools are integrated into the development loop through configuration files that are used by task runners to perform the tasks. By utilizing the task configuration capabilities of Visual Studio Code, developers can continue to work efficiently in a familiar cadence.

8

Unit Testing

➤ Understanding some basic concepts of running unit tests

➤ Learning about the functionality of the Test pane in Visual Studio Code

As was mentioned at the very end of the last chapter, there is a common loop that software developers go through. The edit, compile, test, debug flow is at the heart of what coders do. Most of the book to this point has talked about three of those four steps: editing code, compiling and building the project artifacts, and debugging the application. This leaves us with testing, the topic of this chapter.

TESTING A UNIT

Before drilling down into the support that Visual Studio Code offers for unit testing, let's quickly describe what a unit test is. A *unit*, as we mean it here, is a specific piece of code that we would like to verify works as expected. It could be a method. It could be a class. Either of these works within the definition. The important part is that the functionality of the unit needs to be determined to be correct and, if there are problems, the developer needs to be notified. A *unit test* is a set of code whose purpose is to verify the correctness of the unit.

While it's a little cheesy, there is an acronym frequently associated with what makes a good unit test, TRIP:

Thorough: The set of tests that cover a unit should exercise all the key paths and scenarios. All branches should be tested, a requirement that frequently affects the design of both the methods and classes in your application.

Repeatable: The execution of the tests should produce the same results every time you run it, presuming you didn't modify the code in the interim, of course. What this means from a practical perspective is that you shouldn't be running tests that depend on an external source, like a database or an API call. The database could change, breaking the test, without any change to your application.

Independent: The tests should test one thing and one thing only. It's possible to include multiple assertions in your test, but only one feature or behavior should be covered. As well, the order in which the tests are executed should not matter. A test should not depend on a previous test to set state. If that happens, if something in the test breaks, you'll get multiple error warnings but won't know for sure where the source of the problem is.

Professional: If you are thorough about writing unit tests (and you will be because it's the *T* in TRIP, naturally), you will end up with a large amount of unit testing code. This code is going to be put into source control, along with what you might term *production code*. Except that you should treat the unit code with the same care as production code. Refactor it when necessary. Name the methods consistently and intentionally—all the same steps you take when writing "real" code. Because, whether you realize it or not, unit testing code is just as real and just about as important as production code.

Some people like to include *Automatic* as an attribute of a good unit test. That is to say that the unit tests should be running automatically when you're checking code or before the code gets promoted to the next step in the development pipeline. While it's a very good idea to include an element of automation in the execution of unit tests, there's a much bigger problem. There's no good acronym that includes TRIP and A. So TRIP it is, but work hard toward including Automation.

Visual Studio Code supports unit testing in different ways. First, a couple of languages already have built-in support for unit testing. For example, Python includes a unit test framework in the language and the language service for Python also includes support for PyTest. The catch is that you need to install the Python extension first. For most other languages, unit testing support is not built into the language. Instead, extensions (not language extensions, like Python, but separate components) are available to help. We'll take a look at an extension that allows integration with a number of different unit testing frameworks across different languages.

PYTHON UNIT TESTING

Unit tests are concerned with exercising the surface of an application; that is, the interface—the methods that are exposed, the parameters that are passed, and the values that are returned. They are not concerned with the details of the implementation. While there might occasionally be exceptions to that requirement, they are most definitely the exception and not the rule.

To get started with the unit testing that is built into Python from within Visual Studio Code, you need to install a couple of components. First, from the Extensions pane (see Figure 8-1) search for the Python extension that is from Microsoft and install it.

Once the installation is finished, the extension checks to see if you have Python installed on your machine. If you don't, a notification pops up at the bottom right of the IDE indicating that state and providing a button that, if clicked, takes you to

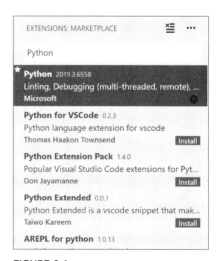

FIGURE 8-1

`https://www.python.org/downloads/`, where you can download the package appropriate for your platform. Download that package, install it, and you should be good for the rest of this example.

So that we have a function to test, create a file called `validatePUI.py` and set the content to the following:

```
import re

def validatePUI(puiName):
    matchObj = re.match(r'^[A-Z]{3}\d{6}$', puiName)
    return matchObj != None
```

This method takes as an incoming parameter the name of a PUI (a practically unique identifier) and validates that it matches a pattern of three capital letters followed by six digits.

Unittest Framework

For this first test example, the built-in Unittest framework will be used, so create a file named `test_unittest.py` and set the contents as follows:

```
import validatePUI
import unittest

class Test_TestValidatePUI(unittest.TestCase):
    def test_validPUI(self):
        self.assertTrue(validatePUI.validatePUI('ABC123456'))

    def test_invalidPUI(self):
        self.assertFalse(validatePUI.validatePUI('ABC12345'))

if __name__ == '__main__':
    unittest.main()
```

To this point, nothing special will have happened in Visual Studio Code. That's because, by default, the Python unit testing frameworks are disabled. To rectify this problem, go to the Settings pane and locate the Python ⇨ Unit Test: Unittest Enabled setting and set it to true. At this point, you'll see a couple of changes in Visual Studio Code. Specifically, you'll see the addition of an icon in the Activity Bar (seen in Figure 8-2).

When you click the icon, the Test: Python view opens up, also shown in Figure 8-2.

By default, the Python extension automatically discovers if there are any unit tests in the current workspace. You can turn this off using the Python ⇨ Unit Test: Auto Test Discover On Saved Enabled setting. But at the moment, if you expand the tree in the Test pane, the unit tests that you added earlier in the example appear (Figure 8-3).

FIGURE 8-2

You execute unit tests through a couple of mechanisms. First, the left icon at the top of the Test pane (the one with the flasks) will launch all the unit tests. If you want to run the unit tests from a single file, click the (green) triangle to the right of the filename. Or you can use the Python: Run All Unit Tests command available through the Command Palette.

When you run the unit tests, you'll see that all of them pass, because the icons turn green (Figure 8-4).

Let's make a small change to a unit test so that a failure can be observed. Modify the second unit test function to be the following, and then run the unit tests again:

```
def test_invalidPUI(self):
    self.assertFalse(validatePUI.validatePUI
('ABC123456'))
```

Now the output looks like Figure 8-5.

You can see that most of what used to be green checkmarks are now red Xs. That's the visual indicator that a test failed during execution. You might also notice that an icon was added at the top, to the right of the Run Unit Tests icon. When this icon is clicked, only the unit tests that failed will be executed.

Finally, when it comes to identifying the reason for a unit test failure, being able to run the test in debug mode is incredibly useful. To do this, click the bug icon (to the right of the Run Unit Tests icon). This will run the unit tests, but if you put breakpoints into your code, execution will pause when they are hit.

The second icon from the right (circular arrow) at the top of the pane is used to rediscover the unit tests in your workspace. If you have enabled the Auto Discover On Save feature, you probably won't need to use this. But if you have turned that off, click this icon to load newly created unit tests into the Tests pane.

The last icon in the pane is used to display the output from the unit test execution (Figure 8-6).

Here you can get more specific details about what went wrong with the unit test, such as which assertion failed.

One additional useful feature of the Python extension is that the unit tests themselves are decorated with a couple of clickable links (see Figure 8-7).

FIGURE 8-3

FIGURE 8-4

FIGURE 8-5

Notice that above both the class definition and the method definitions are two links. One is used to run the test (or tests, in the case of the class). The other is used to debug the test or tests. The X or checkmark to the right of the function indicates the current state (failed or passed) of the test. The goal here is to let you make any changes you might need to a test and rerun it quickly and easily.

PyTest Framework

That last example used the Unittest framework. But the Python extension also includes the PyTest testing framework, so let's see what, if any, difference a change in testing framework makes.

```
PROBLEMS   OUTPUT   DEBUG CONSOLE   TERMINAL          Python Test Log
OK
start
test_unittest.Test_TestValidatePUI.test_invalidPUI
test_unittest.Test_TestValidatePUI.test_validPUI
test_invalidPUI (test_unittest.Test_TestValidatePUI) ... FAIL
NoneType: None
test_validPUI (test_unittest.Test_TestValidatePUI) ... ok

======================================================================
FAIL: test_invalidPUI (test_unittest.Test_TestValidatePUI)
----------------------------------------------------------------------
Traceback (most recent call last):
  File "c:\Users\Bruce Johnson\source\repos\Visual Studio Code\Chapter
  8\Python\test_unittest.py", line 9, in test_invalidPUI
    self.assertFalse(validatePUI.validatePUI('ABC123456'))
AssertionError: True is not false

----------------------------------------------------------------------
Ran 2 tests in 0.008s

FAILED (failures=1)
```

FIGURE 8-6

```
test_unittest.py ×
import validatePUI
import unittest

✗ Run Test | ✗ Debug Test
class Test_TestValidatePUI(unittest.TestCase):
    ✓ Run Test | ✓ Debug Test
    def test_validPUI(self):
        self.assertTrue(validatePUI.validatePUI('ABC123456'))

    ✗ Run Test | ✗ Debug Test
    def test_invalidPUI(self):
        self.assertFalse(validatePUI.validatePUI('ABC123456'))

if __name__ == '__main__':
    unittest.main()
```

FIGURE 8-7

To start, replicate the unit tests for the `validatePUI` method. Create a file called `test_pytest.py`, and set the contents of the file to be the following:

```
import validatePUI

def test_validPUI():
    assert validatePUI.validatePUI('ABC123456')

def test_invalidPUI():
    assert validatePUI.validatePUI('ABC12345') == False
```

If you click the Discover Unit Test icon, nothing will change. That's because the PyTest framework hasn't been enabled. In the Settings, locate the Python ⇨ Unit Test: Py Test Enabled setting and set it to true. Once you have done this, clicking the Discover Unit Test icon will cause the PyTest tests to be added to the pane (see Figure 8-8).

Notice that both the PyTest tests and the Unittest tests are visible. But beyond that, the rest of the user interface is the same. You can run the tests, discover the tests, and debug the tests using the same icons described previously. And, as it turns out, there is nothing (other than, perhaps, a sense of consistency) stopping you from mixing the tests from different frameworks in the same project.

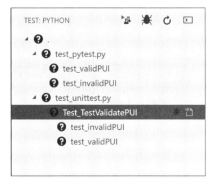

FIGURE 8-8

JAVASCRIPT UNIT TESTING

In this section, we're going to look at a different approach to unit testing within Visual Studio Code. When we get into Chapter 9, "Working with Extensions," we'll mention some of the different unit testing extensions that are available. But, interestingly enough, most of them fit into the same user experience structure as the Python unit tests (that is, there is a Test pane available from the Activity Bar that shows a hierarchy of tests, you can execute or debug the tests from the pane, and the tree that contains the test lights up as red or green depending on the failure or success of the tests).

Instead, for the section on JavaScript unit tests, we'll demonstrate a different approach, one that might give you a better way to stay in the flow while you're writing unit tests.

Jest Extension

For this example, we are going to use the Create-React-App as the base application. Not because the example has any dependencies on React or because you need the functionality of Create-React-App to use the extension. The reason has to do with Jest (like most testing frameworks). Some configuration needs to be done in order to have Jest function, but explaining all of that would unnecessarily add to the length of the book. So instead, start by making sure you have Create-React-App installed on your machine using either npm or yarn. You can find details on not just the application itself, but how to install it at `https://github.com/facebook/create-react-app`. The simplest way to get started for this example is to open a Node.js command prompt and execute the following commands:

```
npx create-react-app js-tests
cd js-tests
code .
```

This creates a directory called `js-tests`, installs Create-React-App, and then uses it to create a new React.js application. Then you change into the newly created directory and launch Visual Studio Code.

Once Visual Studio Code is open, you can see the structure of the project through the Explorer pane. You are going to add a couple of files in the `src` folder.

To start, add a file called `validatePUI.js` and give it the following contents:

```javascript
function validatePUI(puiName) {
    let matchObj = puiName.match(/^[A-Z]{3}\d{6}$/);
    return matchObj != null
}

module.exports = validatePUI;
```

This is the JavaScript (actually, it's really ECMAScript 6, but that's close enough) equivalent of the `validatePUI.py` file from the first section in this chapter.

The second file to add is `validatePUI.test.js`. The contents, shown in the following code, are the unit tests for `validatePUI.js`. It contains the same two tests as you worked with in Python, again translated into JavaScript. The structure of the test is actually using the Jest framework, which is automatically included with Create-React-App:

```javascript
import validatePUI from './validatePUI';

describe('sample JavaScript tests', () => {
  test('validates PUI', () => {
      expect(validatePUI('ABC123456')).toBe(true);
    });

  test('detects invalid PUI', () => {
      expect(validatePUI('ABC12345')).toBe(false);
    });
});
```

The structure of your application should look like the Explorer pane shown in Figure 8-9.

The functionality that is being explored in this section is part of the Jest extension (the full name of the extension is vscode-jest). In the Expansions pane, use **Jest** as the search criterion and select the Jest extension from the list (shown in Figure 8-10).

Click the Install button in the lower-right corner of that extension to install it. After it has been installed, restart Visual Studio Code to initiate the functionality of the extension. The functionality is described in the next few paragraphs.

One of the nice things about this extension is that the current status of the test methods is lit up automatically. As you can see in Figure 8-11, there are colored dots to the left of each test method name. The color of the dots represents the state of the test: a green dot means that the test passed, a red dot indicates a failure, and an uncolored, hollow dot means that the test hasn't been run yet.

FIGURE 8-9

Along with just the color, if a test fails, a number of different indicators are intended to draw your attention to the problem, as well as solve any bugs. Figure 8-12 shows the test code when the test is failing.

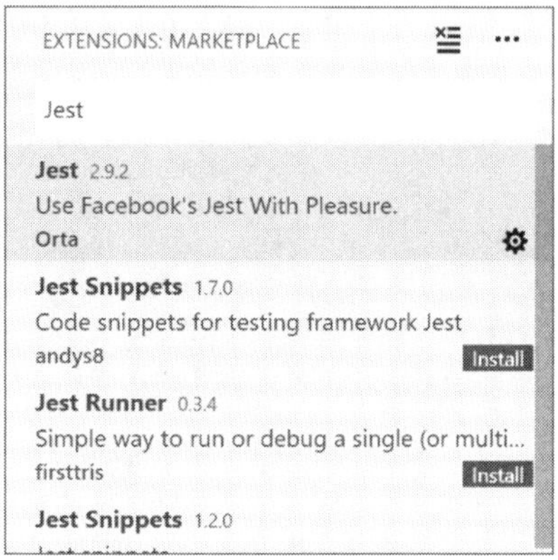

Notice that, along with the red dot, the assertion that is causing the error is underlined with a red squiggle, and a comment has been added to the end of the line with both the expected and actual values retrieved. In addition, there is a Debug link above each method that has an error. Clicking the link will start the unit tests in debug mode.

Also, the errors that were detected by running the unit tests are surfaced in the Problem pane (see Figure 8-13).

Each error is given its own line and the error message contains both the expected and the received values. Clicking any one of the errors navigates to the location in the file where the failing unit test is.

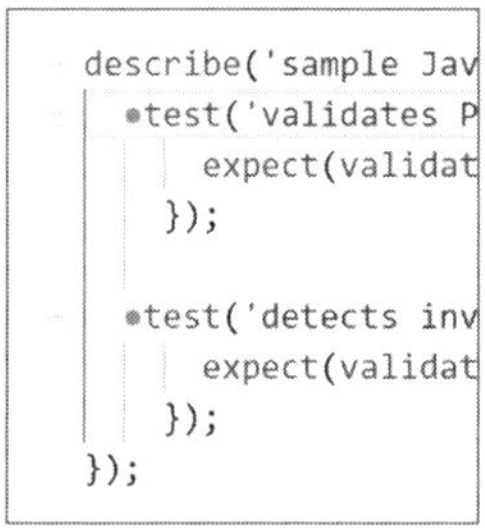

Even the Status Bar gets into the action (see Figure 8-14).

You'll notice the number 2 next to the X icon. That indicates that two problems exist. Clicking that icon reveals the Problems pane. Next to the error and warning icons is a Jest message. If everything is successful, a checkmark will appear to the right of *Jest*. But in this case, there is the warning triangle

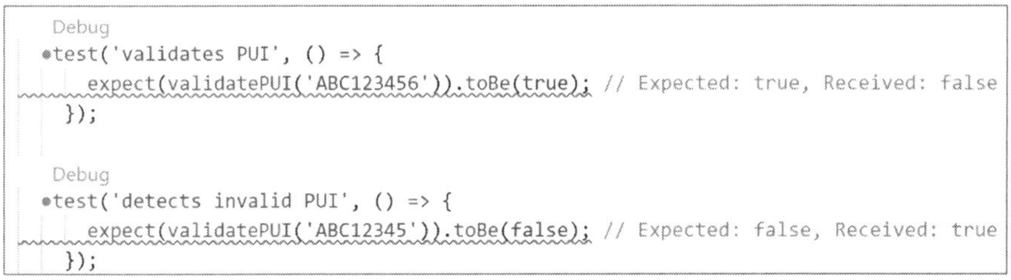

FIGURE 8-10

FIGURE 8-11

```
    Debug
  •test('validates PUI', () => {
      expect(validatePUI('ABC123456')).toBe(true); // Expected: true, Received: false
    });

    Debug
  •test('detects invalid PUI', () => {
      expect(validatePUI('ABC12345')).toBe(false); // Expected: false, Received: true
    });
```

FIGURE 8-12

and a message indicating how many test suites have failed (where *failed* means that at least one test in the suite has failed). If you click the Jest message, the output from the Jest process is displayed in the Terminal pane associated with the extension (see Figure 8-15).

The output that appears in the Terminal pane is basically what you would see if you ran the tests from the command line. In this instance, there are a number of failed tests and each one will have more details about exactly what went wrong and where. If everything is working well with your tests, the messages in this pane will say that as well.

FIGURE 8-13

FIGURE 8-14

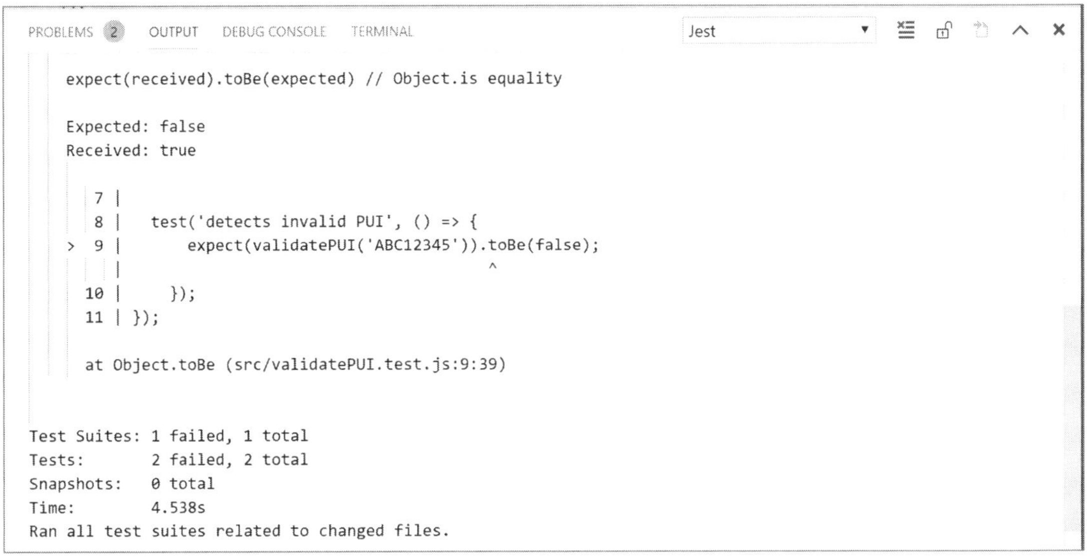

```
PROBLEMS  2    OUTPUT    DEBUG CONSOLE    TERMINAL              Jest           ▼   ⚓ ⬚ ⤢ ∧ ✕

      expect(received).toBe(expected) // Object.is equality

      Expected: false
      Received: true

       7 |
       8 |    test('detects invalid PUI', () => {
     > 9 |        expect(validatePUI('ABC12345')).toBe(false);
         |                                              ^
      10 |    });
      11 | });

      at Object.toBe (src/validatePUI.test.js:9:39)


Test Suites: 1 failed, 1 total
Tests:       2 failed, 2 total
Snapshots:   0 total
Time:        4.538s
Ran all test suites related to changed files.
```

FIGURE 8-15

One of the nice features of this Jest extension is that it is constantly watching for file changes within your workspace. When it detects that a file has changed, it looks at the list of unit tests and determines which unit tests need to be run based on that file. So only those unit tests that might be impacted by the changes you made are executed, and that execution happens automatically. This means that if you make a change that causes a test to break, you find out about it quickly, while the change is still fresh in your mind.

REFACTORING

At the beginning of the chapter, we mentioned the edit, compile, test, debug loop that is a common workflow for developers. The unit testing process has its own loop, known as *red/green/refactor*.

The idea behind this loop is to start by writing a unit test that fails. And more specifically, the reason the test fails is that the functionality necessary for the test to pass has not yet been written. So now when you run the unit test, you'll see a symbol of the failure (an X, a circle, or whatever the unit test extension produces) in red.

Once you have a unit test that fails, you write enough functional code so that that test will pass. This typically is presented within the unit test extension in green. Those two steps are the red and green of the unit testing loop.

The last step, refactor, is a little more complex. As a brief description, refactoring code involves changing the structure of the code without changing its functionality. This could mean anything from adding appropriate line breaks and spacing, to moving code into separate methods, to moving blocks of code that are doing similar functions in different parts of your file into a common method. Ultimately, it's any small, incremental change to your code while keeping what your code does the same.

The purpose of refactoring your code is to improve its readability, modularity, and testability—to clean your code up, to make it, well, better. But in every case, *better* also means that the existing functionality doesn't change, and it's up to the unit tests that you write to ensure this. If you make those small, incremental changes in your code (that is, refactor it), then if the unit tests all work, there have been no changes in functionality. So unit testing and refactoring very much go hand in hand.

Visual Studio Code provides support for the refactoring process. While it doesn't have the ability to evaluate how readable or clean your code is, it does have functions that you can use to make the incremental changes that make up the refactoring. The caveat is that the actual refactoring process is done by the language service, which means that not all languages will have the same set of refactoring options available.

The dependence on the language service makes sense when you consider the process involved. Take a simple refactoring like Extract Method. The basic flow is to select a block of code and start the refactoring. The selected code will be moved to a different part of the file (typically below the current method) and wrapped in a newly created method. The method will be given a name, and the original location for the code will be replaced with a call to that method.

In that description, a lot of assumptions about syntax and structure are implied. For instance, the process doing the refactoring would need to know how to detect the end of the current method (to know where to place the new method), and create a new method, complete with name, parameters, and scoping characters (like curly braces in JavaScript). It would also need to know how to call that method so that the original code can be replaced with a call, including the parameters. All of this is very language-dependent. Having the language service take care of the refactoring functionality makes sense. Now the logic associated with the mechanics of the refactoring is done by a process that has a detailed understanding about the structure of the file and the language. As an added benefit, it means that it's possible for third parties to add their own refactoring functionality to different languages through extensions.

Visual Studio Code includes support for refactoring in JavaScript and TypeScript, but the Marketplace contains extensions that not only add to the standard refactorings offered, but also support refactoring in different languages. What is nice is that the user interface for refactoring is the same across all languages.

Code Actions

In Visual Studio Code, a Code Action is used to trigger both refactoring and quick fixes for issues that have been detected. A quick-fix issue is one that has been highlighted in the code editor with a green squiggle. The availability of a Code Action is indicated by a lightbulb that appears near the source of the problem (see Figure 8-16).

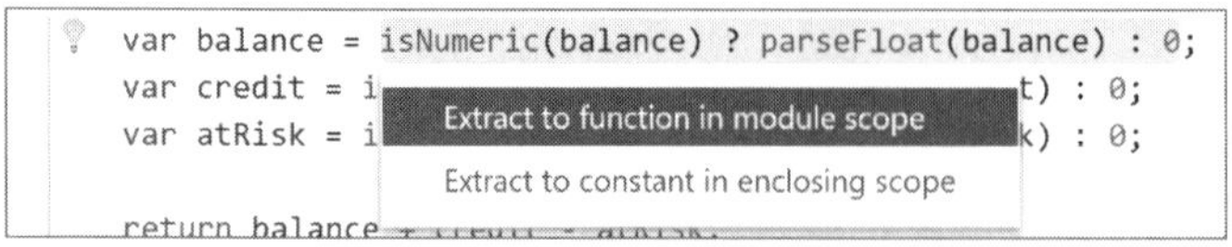

FIGURE 8-16

At the left side of the first line of code, you can see the lightbulb. The list of options, either refactorings or fixes to the code, appears as a drop-down when you click the lightbulb. Alternatively, you can reveal the list by using the Quick Fix command (Ctrl+. by default). If you would prefer to just see the refactorings, you can use the Refactor command, available through the Command Palette, instead.

The actual list of refactorings that are available depends on the context. For the current example, as you can see in Figure 8-16, two options are available, although they are really just variations on the same theme. The names of the refactorings represented by the options are Extract Method and Extract Variable. In both cases, the selected code will be moved to a separate position in the file. The only question is whether it will be converted to a new function or a new constant. For the Extract Method refactoring, the new function would look like the following:

```
function newFunction(balance) {
    return isNumeric(balance) ? parseFloat(balance) : 0;
}
```

Notice that the name of the just-created function is called newFunction. When you click that option in the drop-down, not only is the method created as shown, but you are also prompted for a name for the new method. Figure 8-17 illustrates what that looks like.

```
var balance = newFunction(balance);
var credit = i newFunction       se
var atRisk = isNumeric(atRisk) ? parse
```

FIGURE 8-17

First, notice that the code has already been replaced with a call to the newly created method. Second, when you type a new name in to the text box, the method's name will be changed not only in the line where the method was called, but also where the method is defined. This gives you control over the name for the new method.

```
const newLocal = isNumeric(balance) ? parseFloat(balance) : 0;
var balance = newLocal;
var credit = i newLocal            seFloat(credit) : 0;
var atRisk = isNumeric(atRisk) ? parseFloat(atRisk) : 0;
```

FIGURE 8-18

If you chose the option to create a constant within the current scope (the Extract Variable refactoring), the selected code is converted to the declaration of a new variable (called newLocal by default). Figure 8-18 illustrates the newly created variable.

As with creating a new function, you can change the name of the new constant by entering a value into the text box that appears right below the original code location. This changes the constant's name not only at that location, but also where that constant is defined.

The other refactoring that is supported by Visual Studio Code is Rename Symbol. Unlike the Extract Method and Extract Variable refactorings that are launched through a Code Action (the lightbulb), Rename Symbol is initiated through a Rename Symbol command (by default, using F2 executes that command). In order to be active, you must have selected a variable in your file before using the command. When you press F2, a text box appears below the variable (see Figure 8-19) allowing you to enter a new name.

```
var balance = newLocal;
var balance                 dit)
var atRisk = isNumeric(atRisk)
```

FIGURE 8-19

When you enter the new name, it changes all of the references to that variable within the current file. Appreciate that this is not the same as doing a global replace. The language service that does the refactoring is able to distinguish between when the symbol is being used as variable as opposed to being found in a string. It also recognizes the scope of the variable. So if a variable declared within a method is changed, only the instances of that variable within that method are affected, even if there are identically named variables in different methods.

SUMMARY

The *test* step in the modern develop loop of edit, compile, test, debug is very important. It allows developers to innovate more freely, knowing that changes are not negatively impacting other parts of the application. And having tools that help execute and manage tests is welcome. Not to mention using an editor that includes support for performing refactorings, whether they are built-in or come as part of an extension. All of those factors contribute to the power provided by Visual Studio Code.

In this chapter, we looked at two different approaches to creating and running unit tests. Interestingly, both unit test approaches and refactoring take advantage of extensions and the ecosystem of third-party providers. This leads nicely into the next chapter, which covers how to install and configure extensions in more detail.

Working with Extensions

➤   Understanding how to find, install, and configure extensions

➤   Learning some of the more popular and useful extensions in the Marketplace

One of the main design considerations for Visual Studio Code was extensibility—after creating a top-notch editor experience, that is. Consider the proliferation of frameworks and the speed of growth in the tools that are used to develop applications, web or otherwise. It seems like new versions of Angular, React, and Vue are coming out every month, not to mention new frameworks that are being created or languages that are becoming fashionable. It would be impossible for a single team to be able to keep the tooling for any development environment up to date. The Visual Studio Code team was well aware of this fact. On top of that, its IDE namesake, Visual Studio, has a history of being extensible, dating all the way back to the Visual Basic days of the early 1990s. So allowing extensions was a no-brainer of a decision.

As a result of this approach it's quite likely that, at some point in your development process, you will be using an extension. Extensions support different languages, different testing frameworks, different source control providers, and different syntax and style checking. And, depending on what you're doing, you will choose the extensions that matter to your workflow.

In this chapter, we start by looking at the Extension Marketplace, and discuss how to search for and install extensions. Then we look at some of the most popular or functionally intriguing extensions, just to give you a flavor of what's available and how different extensions approach similar problems.

EXTENSION MARKETPLACE

The starting point for working with extensions in Visual Studio Code is the Extensions pane. The actual contents of the pane depends very much on not just what extensions you might already have installed, but also the kinds of files that you have been opening. Figure 9-1 shows an example of the Extensions pane.

You can open this pane by clicking the Extension icon in the Activity Bar (the square one at the bottom). The contents of the pane itself includes a couple of sections. Visible in Figure 9-1 are collections of recommended and popular extensions. The recommended extensions are based on your activity—the kinds of files you typically open, the features in Visual Studio Code that you use, and other related information gleaned from your use of Visual Studio Code. The star icon in the top-left corner indicates that the extension is recommended, and if you hover over the icon (as seen in Figure 9-2) a tooltip appears telling you why.

The star icon appears on extensions regardless of the section in which they are visible, including any filtering or searching that you perform. If you want, you can turn recommendations off through the Ignore Recommendations setting. With this setting, recommendations won't appear at all. There is also a Show Recommendations Only On Demand setting. If this is turned on, recommendations are only visible if you specifically ask for them by using the @recommended keyword.

The second section visible in Figure 9-1 is a set of popular extensions. This is pretty much exactly what you'd expect: a list of Visual Studio Code extensions that have a large number of installations. It's possible for the Recommended and Popular sections to have overlap (as is evident from the existence of the C# extension in both sections).

FIGURE 9-1

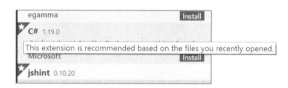

FIGURE 9-2

Not visible in Figure 9-1 are two additional sections: Installed and Disabled. The Installed section contains all the extensions that you have installed, and the Disabled section includes extensions that have been installed but have subsequently been disabled.

Searching for Extensions

While the Recommended and Popular sections are a nice way to find extensions, it is quite likely that they aren't sufficient to find everything you might need. The Extensions pane includes search capabilities that allow you to find extensions in the Visual Studio Code Marketplace. As you enter keywords into the search text box at the top of the pane, the words are used to search the Marketplace. Figure 9-3 illustrates the result when *JavaScript* is used as the keyword.

The Visual Studio Code Marketplace is a clearinghouse for extensions written by a wide variety of people. It's like an App Store for extensions. If you want to see the web experience, you can find the Marketplace at `https://marketplace .visualstudio.com/VSCode`.

Along with keyword searching, you have a couple of options available to sort the results. To quickly see what the syntax looks like, click the ellipsis at the top right of the Extensions pane (see Figure 9-4).

About halfway down the menu on the right, you will notice three sorting options: By Install Count, By Rating, and By Name. If you click any of these options, the text used to provide the search criteria is modified slightly (see Figure 9-5) and the results are sorted accordingly.

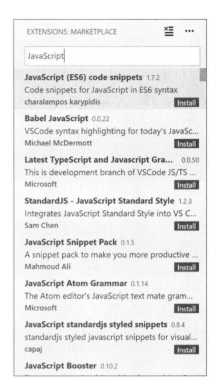

FIGURE 9-3

FIGURE 9-4

FIGURE 9-5

You'll notice the addition of the @sort keyword, followed by an additional qualifier. The qualifier indicates the type of sort. Figure 9-5 uses the *name* qualifier. The other options shown in Figure 9-4 would result in qualifiers of *installs* and *rating*.

The use of the @sort keyword introduces a pattern that Visual Studio Code uses to help you pare down your list of results. A number of keywords that are prefixed with an at symbol are available to you. To see a list, clear out the search criteria text box and then type an **@** (Figure 9-6).

FIGURE 9-6

As you can see from Figure 9-6, many keywords are available. The first six (`@builtin`, `@disabled`, `@enabled`, `@installed`, `@outdated`, `@recommended`) are items that can be found in the menu displayed in Figure 9-4. The three `@sort` plus qualifier options are visible as well. But there are a couple of other choices, some visible, some not, that you can use:

> `@ext`—Theoretically, this would look for extensions that are associated with a particular language. At the moment, this keyword does not appear to work.

> `@tag`—Also a nonfunctional tag, but it should search for extensions based on a tag. Each extension, when published, can identify tags that apply to it. Examples are terms like *format*, *json*, and *debugger*. When this keyword works, you will be using the qualifier to match against the specified tags.

> `@category`—Not unlike `@tag` in the idea that extensions include the category to which they belong when they are published. Using this keyword will filter based on extensions whose category matches the specified qualifier. The difference is that while an extension can choose any tag (and any number of tags), each extension can only choose categories from a predefined list. Figure 9-7 illustrates the different categories that can be used.

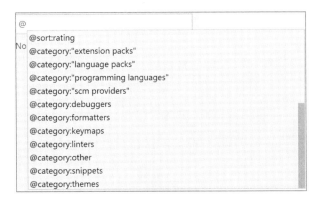

FIGURE 9-7

The category for an extension also impacts how it gets displayed within the web version of the Visual Studio Code Marketplace. While a generic search functionality is available, there is also a treelike navigation structure that allows you to view the extensions that are in each of the categories.

Installing Extensions

Once you have found an extension you want to use, the next step is to install it. Visual Studio Code makes it easy to install extensions. But first, you might want to see some detailed information about the extension. When you click any of the extensions in the pane, an editor window containing some details of the extension appears in the current editor group.

Figure 9-8 shows an example of the details for the C# extension. If you were to look at the web page for the C# extension in the Visual Studio Code Marketplace website, you'd see a very high level of correlation. That's because what you see in the editor is a variation of the web page for the extension.

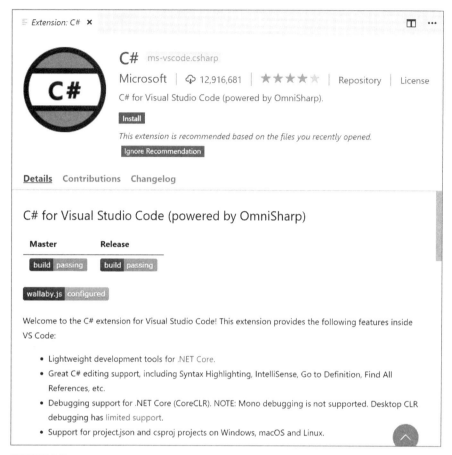

FIGURE 9-8

What appears on this page depends on the extension author. However, some basic pieces of information are available for all extensions. At the top, you can see the name for the extension (both the full name and the user-friendly name), the description, the name of the author, the number of installations, the current rating, and links to the repository and the license.

The information in the Details pane is entirely up to the author, with just a couple of exceptions. However, those exceptions are not visible on this pane, but on the extension's website in the Marketplace.

If you click the name of the extension at the top of the Details pane (the C# in Figure 9-8), the web page for the extension opens. As was already mentioned, the contents of the web page mimic the contents of the Details pane pretty closely. The main exception is on the right side of the overview. Here, you'll see some additional details for the extension (as shown in Figure 9-9).

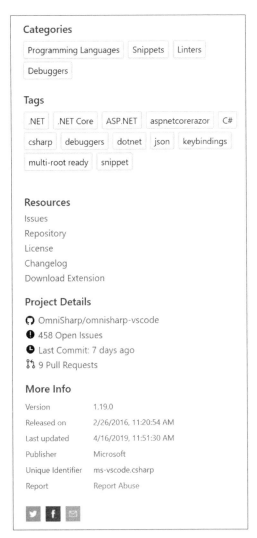

FIGURE 9-9

You can see the categories to which the extension belongs, and the tags that are associated with the extension. There is information about the version and release dates, the name of the publisher, and links to the license for the extension. If the publisher is using GitHub to host the source code, more detailed information about the project is also displayed. This includes a link to the main GitHub page, the number of open issues, the number of outstanding pull requests, and how recently the last commit was made. This information can be quite handy when trying to determine if you want to install an extension or not. One of the dangers of any third-party component is that support for it languishes. That can happen because the author changes jobs, moves on to another project, or the component has just become stable with little need for changes. The information available on the website can help determine the current status of the extension; for example, recent commits indicate active development, and a low number of open issues suggests stability. Pull requests, which are made by developers hoping to contribute to the project, are also a decent indicator of health and community interest.

From within Visual Studio Code, installing an extension is basically clicking a button. In the Details pane for any extension, there is an Install button toward the top. Alternatively, in the Extensions pane, each of the listed extensions not currently installed has an Install button in the bottom right (see Figure 9-10).

FIGURE 9-10

Clicking either of those buttons starts the installation process. That process involves downloading the extension from the Marketplace, installing it, and, if necessary, asking the user to restart Visual Studio Code.

On the web page for the extension, there is also a Download Extension link. Clicking this link allows you to download the VSIX (Visual Studio Interface Extension) package. You don't need to do this in order to install the extension in most cases, but in some instances it is necessary.

Once installed, the Extensions pane view, along with the Details pane, changes slightly (see Figure 9-11).

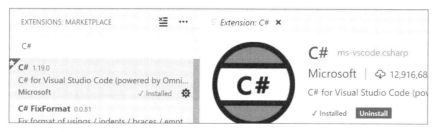

FIGURE 9-11

In the Extensions pane, the Install button has become a message indicating that the extension is installed, and a gear icon, when clicked, exposes the options available to manage the extension. In the Details pane for the extension, the caption on the Install button has changed to Installed, and there is now a button that can be used to uninstall the extension.

There is another option for installing extensions into Visual Studio Code, which is to work directly with the VSIX file. Even when an extension is in the Marketplace, reasons exist for why you might need to work directly with a VSIX file. For example, the network security policies of some companies restrict the sites that are accessible. Or, they require that the user performing an installation have administrator rights, but restrict the administrators from having access to the Internet.

Regardless of the reason, the premise is that you have access to the VSIX file, but not to the Marketplace. In the menu that is available through the ellipsis in the Expansions pane (see Figure 9-4), there is an Install From VSIX option. When this option is selected, a File Open dialog appears allowing you to navigate to and choose the VSIX file. Click the Open button and the installation process starts. Once the installation is complete, you can manage the extension through the same interfaces as any other extension.

Extension Configuration

Extensions can provide their own configuration settings. Visual Studio Code provides the hooks necessary for extensions to surface those settings through the standard interface. Figure 9-12 shows the Settings page.

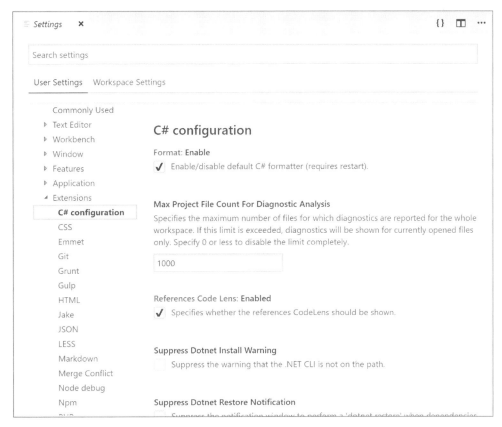

FIGURE 9-12

On the left side, one of the navigation elements is Extensions. This is where you can find the settings related to installed extensions. In this example, the configuration for the C# extension has been selected, and on the right are the settings for that extension. Each of the extensions will have its own settings. In some cases, you can see the list of settings for an extension on the Contributions page in the Details pane for the extension. Figure 9-13 shows an example for the C# extension, but the basic choices for the user interface for the settings are the same regardless of whether it's Visual Studio Code or a third-party extension.

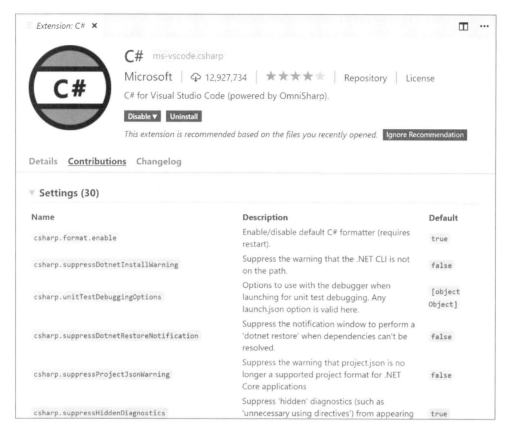

FIGURE 9-13

The Contributions tab in the Details pane also includes other areas where an extension has added to the Visual Studio Code experience. For example, consider Figure 9-14.

This is the Contributions tab for the C# extension with some of the sections collapsed. You can see that, beyond settings, a number of other items are added to Visual Studio Code by the extension. For example, commands are added that are available through the Command Palette. It has added support for two different languages in two different ways. For C#, it has added some snippets. For ASP. NET Core Razor, it has added syntactical understanding so that the files (`*.cshtml` and `*.razor`) can be colored appropriately. It has added support so that IntelliSense is active in `project.json` and `omnisharp.json` files, and it has added debugging support for .NET and .NET Core. Again, how each extension modifies Visual Studio Code will be different. Not all the possible additions are shown in Figure 9-14, but this should give you a sense for the depth of integration that is possible for extensions.

FIGURE 9-14

While technically not configuration, Visual Studio Code allows you to enable and disable extensions should the need arise. The reasons for doing this are varied. Perhaps an extension is causing poor performance, or the extension is not needed for the project that you'll be spending the majority of your time on. Regardless of the rationale, disabling and re-enabling is a straightforward process.

In the Expansions pane, locate the extension you'd like to disable. When you click the gear icon, the menu shown in Figure 9-15 appears. Notice that there are two Disable options: the first, Disable, disables the extension for all of Visual Studio Code, and the second, Disable (Workspace), just disables the extension in the current workspace.

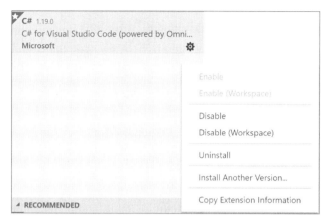

FIGURE 9-15

Once an extension is disabled, it appears in a different section of the Extensions pane. To re-enable the extension, click the gear icon for the extension and choose either the Enable or Enable (Workspace) options from the menu (seen faintly in Figure 9-15; they are not grayed out if the extension has been disabled).

If you're done with the extension, the menu displayed by clicking the gear icon also includes an Uninstall option.

All three of these functions can also be performed through a button on the Details pane for the extension. Figure 9-16 shows the Disable and Uninstall buttons.

FIGURE 9-16

Updating Extensions

By default, Visual Studio Code automatically updates extensions when new versions are available. If the update requires that Visual Studio Code be restarted, you'll be notified through a toast message in the bottom right of the IDE.

You can change the default behavior through two settings. The Auto Update setting controls whether Visual Studio Code will automatically update extensions. If this is turned off, extensions will appear in the Outdated section instead of being updated. But that means that Visual Studio Code is still checking (a Microsoft service is called when looking for updates). If you'd rather that Visual Studio Code not even check for updates, set the Auto Check Updates setting to false.

If you turn off automatic updates, and you decide you want to update your extensions, you can access the mechanism to do so through the ellipsis menu in the Extensions pane. Click the Check For Extension updates option to start the process of getting the update information from the Microsoft service that manages delivering updates. Once that information is available, the extensions that have an update appear in the Outdated section. Clicking the Update button will update that extension. To update all your extensions, use the Update All Extensions command available in the Command Palette.

Workspace Extensions

As you might have deduced from the fact that extensions can be enabled or disabled for a specific workspace, it's possible to define extensions that are associated with a given workspace. In other words, an extension is disabled for one workspace but when you open a different workspace, the extension is enabled.

One additional piece of functionality related to extensions and workspaces helps greatly if you're working in a team environment. It's possible to define a set of recommended extensions for a workspace. That information is stored in a JSON file and is included with the workspace files. When another developer opens the workspace, the list of recommended extensions will include the extensions that you defined for that workspace.

To create this file, use the Extensions: Configure Recommended Extensions (Workspace) command. This command creates a file called `extensions.json` in the `.vscode` folder. The structure of the file is as follows:

```
{
    "recommendations": [
        "dbaeumer.vscode-eslint",
        "msjsdiag.debugger-for-chrome"
    ],
    "unwantedRecommendations": [
        "ms-vscode.vscode-typescript-tslint-plugin"
    ]
}
```

Each of the elements in the `recommendations` array (or the `unwantedRecommendations` array) is the fully qualified name of an extension. The form of a fully qualified name is *publisher. extensionName*. You can find the name for any extension in the Details pane. For example, Figure 9-17 shows the details for the ESLint extension, and you can see that the name found in the Recommendations section above has been highlighted.

FIGURE 9-17

Just to close the loop on the functionality, any extension in the `recommendations` array will be included in the Recommendations section for a person opening the workspace. Conversely, if an extension appears in the `unwantedRecommendations` array, then it will not appear in the Recommendations section, even if it would have been recommended based on the user's history. In the example, the ESLint and Debugger for Chrome extension would be recommended, but the TSLint extension would not be.

If you are using a multi-root workspace, then instead of an `extensions.json` file, the recommendations and unwanted recommendations appear in the `code-workspace` file. In that case, there would be `extensions.recommendations` and `extensions.unwantedRecommendations` arrays in the JSON file, similar to the following:

```
{
    "extensions": {
        "recommendations": [
```

```
            "dbaeumer.vscode-eslint",
            "msjsdiag.debugger-for-chrome"
        ],
        "unwantedRecommendations": [
            "ms-vscode.vscode-typescript-tslint-plugin",
        ]
    }
}
```

Command-Line Interface

If you are trying to automate the configuration of Visual Studio Code, the fact that a command-line interface is available can be a saving grace. Through the command line, you can display the installed extensions, see the current version of these extensions, and install or uninstall an extension. The options to accomplish this are as follows:

```
code --list-extensions
```

Lists out the currently installed extensions.

```
code --list-extensions --show-versions
```

Includes the current version information for each of the installed extensions.

```
code --install-extension <extensionId>
```

Installs the specified extension. The `<extensionId>` is the fully qualified extension name.

```
code --install-extension extensionName.vsix
```

Installs an extension. The `extensionName.vsix` is the path to the VSIX file for the extension. This form of the command allows you to automate the installation of an extension from a local share.

```
code --uninstall-extension <extensionId>
```

Uninstalls the specified extension. The `<extensionId>` is the fully qualified extension name.

```
code --disable-extensions
```

Disables all the currently installed extensions.

```
code --disable-extension <extensionId>
```

Disables the specified extension. The `<extensionId>` is the fully qualified extension name.

```
code --install-extension <extensionId>
```

Installs the specified extension. The `<extensionId>` is the fully qualified extension name.

USEFUL EXTENSIONS

The sheer volume of extensions can be quite daunting. More importantly, the ones that matter to you depend on your coding style and the type of projects that you're working with. Still, it's worthwhile to list of some of the extensions that not only are popular, but address common issues—especially if those issues cross over different languages. So with that objective in mind, the following sections discuss some of the extensions that are available in the Marketplace that fit into the category of "must look at."

Linters

How can I resist? A linter is a machine that removes the short fibers from cotton seeds after ginning. And here you thought you'd learn nothing useful from the book.

Okay, seriously, in the world of development, a linter is a tool that helps to verify the quality of the code that has been written. It checks for formatting discrepancies, ensures that your code adheres to predefined standards, and checks for possible logical errors—all of which is a positive when it comes to producing reliable code.

The following Visual Studio Code extensions perform linting. Because linters are language-dependent, you'll find different ones for the different languages:

➤ *TSLint (eg2.tslint)*—There are two versions of this extension: one marked deprecated and one that replaces the deprecated one. Interestingly, people have been having issues getting the newest one to work properly. So until those issues have been worked out, you might want to stick with the deprecated version.

➤ *ESLint (dbaeumer.vscode-eslint)*—Integrates the open-source project called ESLint into Visual Studio Code. This linter is aimed at JavaScript and JSX.

➤ *SASS Lint (glen-84.sass-lint)*—Provides linting functions for SASS.

➤ *markdownlint (DavidAnson.vscode-markdownlint)*—Linting functionality for the Markdown markup language.

➤ *JSHint (dbaeumer.jshint)*—Like ESLint, JSHint targets JavaScript. Also like ESLint, this is the integration of an open-source module into Visual Studio Code. But in this case, the module is JSHint.

Keyboard Mappings

If you're coming from a different editor, getting up to speed on the default Visual Studio Code keyboard shortcuts is annoying, and it slows productivity. A good keyboard mapper takes the shortcuts that you're comfortable with and automatically applies them to Visual Studio Code:

➤ *Visual Studio Keymap (ms-vscode.vs-keybindings)*—Ports popular keyboard mappings from Visual Studio to Visual Studio Code. The mappings are not perfect (Visual Studio Code doesn't implement all of the shortcuts that Visual Studio does), but it provides a level of familiarity for Visual Studio users.

➤ *Vim (vscodevim.vim)*—Provides Vim emulation for Visual Studio Code.

➤ *Sublime Text Keymap (ms-vscode.sublime-keybindings)*—Ports a set of popular Sublime Text keyboard shortcuts to Visual Studio Code.

➤ *Atom Keymap (ms-vscode.sublime-keybindings)*—Ports a set of popular Atom keyboard shortcuts to Visual Studio Code.

➤ *EditorConfig for Visual Studio Code (EditorConfig.EditorConfig)*—Uses the settings found in the `.editorconfig` file to update the shortcuts in Visual Studio Code. EditorConfig is a cross-language configuration tool that provides a consistent set of shortcuts across file types and editors.

Snippets and Coding Assistance

Helping you write code fast is what editors are supposed to do. If you look through the Marketplace, you'll find a lot of snippet extensions. That's because, in general, snippet extensions are pretty easy to implement by the component authors, so they are decent places to try out the process (themes are the other hotbed for novice publishers). But some extensions in this category are definitely worth your time:

➤ *React-Native/React/Redux snippets for es6/es7 (EQuimper.react-native-react-redux)*—React, Redux, React Native all in one set of snippets.

➤ *Angular 8 Snippets (Mikael.Angular-BeastCode)*—A collection of Angular-related snippets that support versions of Angular all the way up to version 8.

➤ *Angular v7 Snippets (johnpapa.Angular2)*—Also a collection of Angular-related snippets, but the extension has only been updated through version 7.

➤ *HTML CSS Support (ecmel.vscode-html-css)*—Provides support for automatic completion of class and ID attributes. Also has the ability to include remote CSS files in its processing.

➤ *jQuery Code Snippets (donjayamanne.jquerysnippets)*—A collection of snippets for jQuery projects.

Miscellaneous Tools

Some of the most interesting extensions don't fall neatly into a specific category. First, a wide variety of languages have their own extensions (and are supported within Visual Studio Code for syntax checking, auto completion, and sometimes even execution purposes). That list would be too long, but if you want support for a particular obscure language, the existence of an extension is frequently sufficient cause for excitement.

But even beyond languages, some extensions are just flat-out useful for helping you debug applications, improve performance, ease deploying, or just make your development life easier:

➤ *SQL Server (mssql) (ms-mssql.mssql)*—Sorry for the confusing name, but the actual name of the extension includes the parentheses. This extension gives you the ability to connect to a SQL Server data store (locally or in Azure), execute queries against the database, and view the results. Consider it to be a lightweight SQL Server Management Studio and you're pretty close.

➤ *Debugger for Chrome (msjsdiag.debugger-for-chrome)*—Allows you to debug your JavaScript while running through the Chrome browser. Functionality includes breakpoints, stepping, watches, locals, and a console window.

➤ *Docker (PeterJausovec.vscode-docker)*—Working with containers is a very common task for developers, especially as the world of DevOps and continuous deployment becomes more commonplace. If you work with Docker, this extension is a joy. It will do syntax highlighting and linting on the Docker configuration files. The Command Palette includes most common Docker commands, and there is integration with Explorer for managing images and running containers. The only downside (and if you use Docker, this probably won't even slow you down) is that you need to have Docker installed on your system to take advantage of it.

➤ *GitLens (eamodio.gitlens)*—While support for Git is built into Visual Studio Code, there are still some areas for improvement. This extension helps to fill in the gaps. Specifically, it exposes information about the history of a file through a series of code decorations. This includes code lens functionality (the links that appear above lines of code), gutter decoration (icons and colors that appear in the margins of the code editor), and Status Bar messages. In addition, it adds a side bar that makes it is easier for you to navigate through the information that is available within Git repositories.

➤ *Rest Client (humao.rest-client)*—The basic functionality of this extension is to allow you to send HTTP requests and view the response. But in that single statement is a lot of usefulness. You can easily use this extension to run tests against an API endpoint, a SOAP endpoint, or any HTTP endpoint. Multiple commands in a single file are possible, and the commands themselves are available through either a history view or having previously been saved. Code snippets for submitting HTTP requests are also available in a number of languages.

➤ *Import Cost (wix.vscode-import-cost)*—One of the challenges of developing web applications for mobile devices is the size of the files that are included. It's very easy to add a new package to your project. It's just as easy to use the one method in that package that you required. What isn't obvious is how much your application's download size increased with that one action. The purpose of Import Cost is to make that impact visible to the developer. It lets the developers see how much size was added so that they can, say, place a monetary value on their solution to the one time they need to format currency, because an increased download size can have an impact on people using your applications. Having that information might not necessarily change the decision, but at least the choice is being made with eyes open.

➤ *Bracket Pair Colorizer 2 (CoenraadS.bracket-pair-colorizer-2)*—In a world of monochromatic brackets, how can you easily see which brackets match with which? Yes, if you click a bracket, the default functionality for many languages is to highlight its companion. But that requires a click. The goal of this extension is to eliminate that click by using different colors to indicate the match. This way, you can see which brackets match up without changing the cursor position. Note that two extensions have similar names—Bracket Pair Colorizer and Bracket Pair Colorizer 2. The most popular (at this time) is the older one, Bracket Pair Colorizer, but the new one, Bracket Pair Colorizer 2, is from the same author and includes some improvements that broke the old version. Hence, a new extension was created. But the basic functionality is the same in both cases.

SUMMARY

The extension ecosystem for Visual Studio Code is quite vibrant. New additions to the Marketplace are constantly being added. While not all of these additions are going to be useful, it's a solid bet that some of them will become priceless parts of your development flow. And that's really what's important.

In this chapter, we looked at how to find, install, and manage extensions. In addition, we described some of the most commonly useful and popular extensions. The ability to create extensions is powerful, especially if you're trying to add functionality that is custom to your job but also useful to the rest of your team. In the next chapter, we look at how to go about creating your own extension for Visual Studio Code.

10

Creating Your Own Extensions

WHAT'S IN THIS CHAPTER?

➤   Understanding how to create a Visual Studio Code extension

➤   Learning how to define the contributions made by your extensions

➤   Integrating extensions into the existing Visual Studio Code user experience

As the previous chapter should have reinforced, Visual Studio Code is quite extensible, and third-party authors (not to mention Microsoft) are taking advantage of that extensibility to create a wide range of useful extensions. But, almost inevitably, you will find things that are missing in Visual Studio Code or features you'd like added to help you or your team, so it makes sense to spend a bit of time looking at the details of how extensions are constructed.

The goal of this chapter is to walk you through the process of setting up a simple extension: examining the structure of an extension project, working with the different points of extension that are offered within Visual Studio Code, and considering how debugging an extension works.

GETTING STARTED

While it's certainly possible to write a Visual Studio Code extension from scratch, it's a lot easier to utilize Yeoman and a code generator that has been provided.

If you're unfamiliar with Yeoman, it is a scaffolding tool. Its purpose is to create the starting point for projects of various types. It's language agnostic, because it's not actually compiling anything. It just creates the directory structure, adds the appropriate files, and off you go. If you haven't installed Yeoman on your machine, you can do so with the following command from a Bash command shell:

```
npm install -g yo
```

Once you have installed Yeoman, you also need to install the generator for Visual Studio Code extensions. It is called generator-code, and you can install it with the following command:

```
npm install -g generator-code
```

Now that the pieces are installed, let's scaffold the extension. Still in the Bash shell, execute the following command:

```
yo code
```

You are now going to be asked a bunch of questions about the extension you're creating. The starting point is to identify the type of extension you want. Figure 10-1 shows the list of extensions that are available in this scaffold:

➤ *Color Theme*—Visual Studio Code allows you to define a color theme and package it as an extension. Once the extension is installed, you can use it through the File ⇨ Preferences ⇨ Color Theme option.

➤ *Extension (TypeScript or JavaScript)*— Each of these is a project that contains a generic extension. The only difference is the language used to write the functionality.

➤ *Extension Pack*—An extension pack is a collection of (presumably) related extensions that will be installed as a single unit.

➤ *Keymap*—Defines a specific keyboard mapping, usually with the intent of having the keyboard commands for Visual Studio Code mimic the keyboard commands for another editor (such as Notepad++, Sublime Text, or Visual Studio).

➤ *Language Pack*—Contains the localized string resources for a specific language (if you wanted your Visual Studio Code interface to be in Klingon, for example).

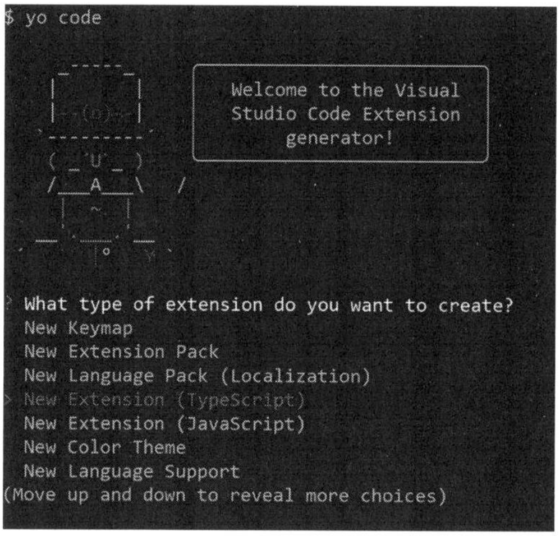

FIGURE 10-1

As you can see, it contains quite a few choices. But for the sample in this chapter, choose Extension (TypeScript) to get started. The next step for each of the choices varies. However, the first three pieces of information are the same:

➤ *Name*—The name of the extension. This is the name that will be viewed by users of the Marketplace. It is not a requirement that the name be unique, but you should probably check to see if it is already being used.

➤ *Identifier*—The identifier of the extension. This name does need to be unique, but it doesn't need to be user-friendly. There also can be no spaces in the identifier. You'll see the identifier used when including extensions in extension packs, workspace recommendations, and wherever you need to be precise about identifying an extension.

➤ *Description*—A description for the extension. This should include a description of the goal, functionality, and purpose of the extension.

Beyond these attributes, the set of information you need to provide depends on the type of extension you selected. For instance, if you choose Extension Pack, there is nothing more you need to provide. But if you choose Extension (like you did), you will need to give some additional details. Figure 10-2 shows the set of questions that are required for an extension.

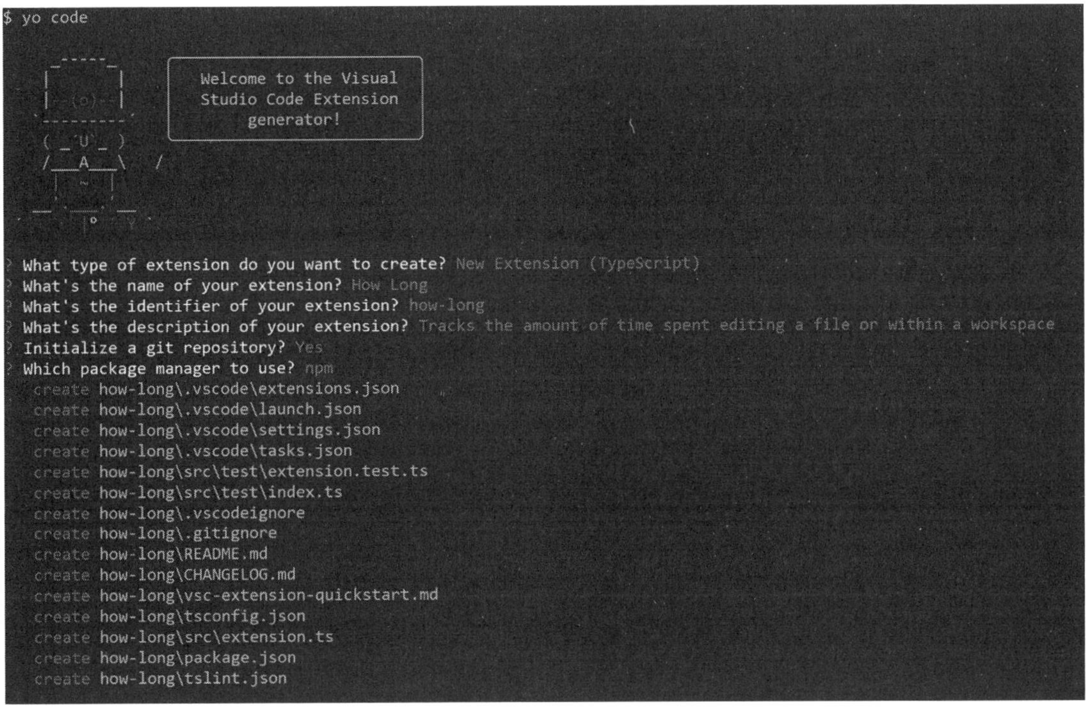

FIGURE 10-2

The answers that are shown in Figure 10-2 for the two additional questions are the default values. But if you choose different answers, it shouldn't have any impact on you working through the sample in this chapter.

When you have answered the questions, Yeoman goes to work. It creates the appropriate folder structure and adds the required files. Once that is done, it runs a command to install all of the necessary components (either an `npm install` or `yarn install`). And now you're ready to go. To run your new extension, change directory into the just created folder and launch Visual Studio Code:

```
cd how-long
code .
```

Once Visual Studio Code is loaded, you'll see a notification message appear in the bottom right of the IDE (Figure 10-3).

FIGURE 10-3

The reason for this message is that the scaffolded project includes a recommendation for the TSLint extension. You can choose to install it, view the list of recommended extensions, or just ignore the message. If you already have TSLint installed, you wouldn't see this message.

Interestingly, in order for an extension to be tested, a second instance of Visual Studio Code needs to be running. One instance is where you are currently developing; the second instance is where your extension will be deployed and where you can test it.

To run your extension, use the Debug ⇨ Start Debugging menu option. After a few moments, you'll see a new instance of Visual Studio Code launched. The most visible differences between the new *testing* instance and the one you were developing in are that the testing instance (known officially as the development host) has no workspace opened when you launch, and the title bar includes the phrase *[Extension Development Host]*. This testing instance is the one currently running your extension.

To try out the functionality of your extension, open the Command palette (View ⇨ Command Palette) and execute the command `Hello World`. A toast message appears in the bottom right of the IDE (see Figure 10-4). This is the functionality implemented in the scaffolded project.

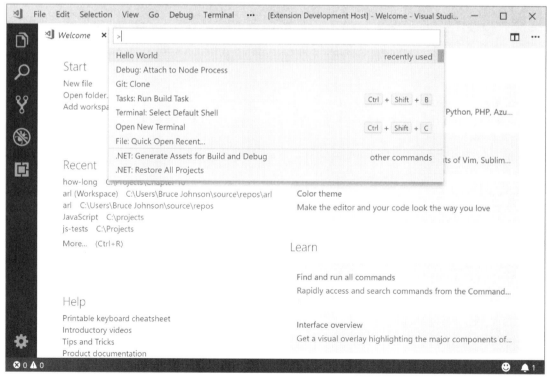

FIGURE 10-4

Visual Studio Code supports debugging while running your extensions in the development host instance. In your originally running instance, open the `extension.ts` file and set a breakpoint on line 20 (the call to `vscode.window.showInformationMessage`). Then go back to the development host instance and execute the **Hello World** command again. Your code will pause at the breakpoint, just as you would expect (Figure 10-5).

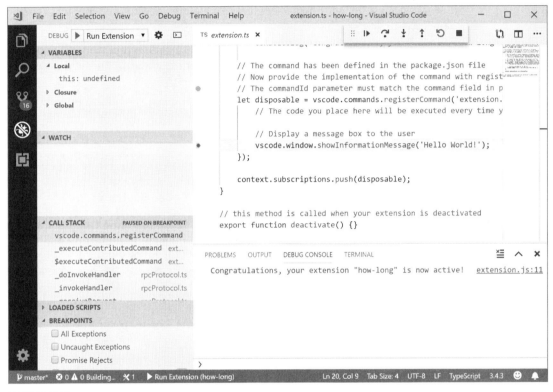

FIGURE 10-5

The thrust of this demonstration is that you can consider coding, testing, and debugging the extension to be pretty much the same as any other platform. The only significant difference is that while running your extension, it has to be executing within the context of an instance of Visual Studio Code.

In the next section, we look at the anatomy of that project and start to look at how to work with the extensibility points provided by Visual Studio Code.

AN EXTENSION PROJECT

To get a handle on the workings of the sample extension, it's important to understand the following three concepts:

➤ *Activation events*—Visual Studio Code has a collection of events that get raised at certain times while it is being used (for example, when a command is executed from the Command Palette). When an event is raised, it can, in turn, cause an extension to become active.

The list of possible events is covered in the "Activation Events" section later in this chapter, but for the sample project, the onCommand activation event is the trigger.

➤ *Contribution points*—A static list, in the package.json file, of all of the contributions that are made by the extension project. In the parlance of Visual Studio Code, a *contribution* is a piece of functionality that is added to Visual Studio Code, such as a command, a keystroke mapping, or a menu item. The possible contribution points are discussed in the "Contribution Points" section later in this chapter.

➤ *Visual Studio Code API*—A collection of APIs that can be called from the JavaScript within your extension. It is typically through this API that your extension will interface with Visual Studio Code during runtime.

So with an eye to these three areas, let's look at what the sample extension is actually doing.

Activation Event

An activation event is an event that occurs within Visual Studio Code that triggers the activation of an extension. As was already mentioned, the activation event that is used by the sample is onCommand. What this means is that when a specific command is executed, the extension is activated.

What determines the relationship between the command and the extension? That's a setting in the package.json file that associates the extension with a specific command. Open up the package .json file and look for the activationEvents array. It looks like the following.

```
"activationEvents": [
    "onCommand:extension.helloWorld"
],
```

The onCommand portion is the name of the activation event. extension.helloWorld is the name of the command that triggers the activation event.

Contribution Points

Defining an activation event for onCommand isn't going to do anything to add the command to Visual Studio Code. For that, extensions depend on contribution points.

The term *contribution* might seem a little odd. It's a completely accurate description, but is not a commonplace usage of the word in the software world. Consider it as follows. Visual Studio Code is a collection of user-interface features: menus, commands, keyboard shortcuts, and other user-interface elements. Your extension is going to contribute its own set of user-interface elements to the collection of elements that Visual Studio Code has. Hence, the term *contribution* makes sense. A contribution point is one of the places in Visual Studio Code where a contribution can be made.

For a particular extension, the list of contributions is found as a static declaration made in the package.json file. Consider the following section from the package.json file in the sample extension:

```
"contributes": {
    "commands": [
        {
            "command": "extension.helloWorld",
            "title": "Hello World"
        }
    ]
}
```

The `contributes` attribute is a JSON object. Each of the attributes in the object has a name that indicates the part of Visual Studio Code to which the contribution will be made. In the example, the extension is going to add a command. Specifically, it is going to add a command with a title of Hello World. That means that in the Command Palette, you will execute Hello World to trigger the command, and the command that gets triggered is `extension.helloWorld`.

Visual Studio Code API

So now Visual Studio Code knows that it activates the extension on a command called `extension.helloWorld`, and it has added a user-interface command called Hello World that will trigger the `extension.helloWorld` command. The last step is to connect that command to actual functionality in your extension.

To accommodate this, Visual Studio Code exposes a collection of endpoints. The endpoints are available to your extension through JavaScript and TypeScript functions. For the sample extension, the *commands* namespace contains functions that are used to define that link. In the sample extension, open the `extension.ts` file. You'll see an `activate` method that looks like the following (after the comments and log statements have been removed):

```
export function activate(context: vscode.ExtensionContext) {
    let disposable = vscode.commands.registerCommand('extension.helloWorld',
        () => {
            vscode.window.showInformationMessage('Hello World!');
        });

    context.subscriptions.push(disposable);
}
```

The `activate` method is a method that every extension exposes. It is executed the first (and only the first) time the extension is activated.

Inside the `activate` method, it uses the `commands` object to register a handler for the `extension.helloWorld` command. Then that registration is pushed into the list of subscriptions for Visual Studio Code. Now when the `extension.helloWorld` command is triggered, the anonymous method that calls `showInformationMessage` is invoked, which causes the Hello World message to appear in a toast message. This is the functionality that the extension intended to produce.

Extension Project Structure

Now that the functionality in the sample extension has been covered, let's take a look at the structure and components that were added to the extension project when it was scaffolded. Interestingly, only two files (`package.json` and `extension.ts`) were involved in the implementation. The rest of the files are there to support testing, configuration of the supporting tools, and documentation. Figure 10-6 shows the project structure.

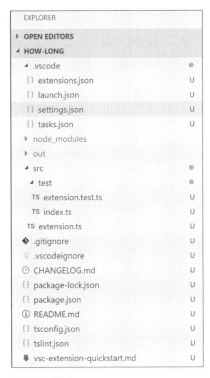

FIGURE 10-6

Starting from the top, you see a `.vscode` folder. This folder contains configuration files for different parts of Visual Studio Code. In Figure 10-6, there are four configuration files:

➤ `extensions.json`—Configures the extensions being used in this workspace, specifically the recommendations and unwanted recommendations.

➤ `launch.json`—Contains the launch options for the projects. Two launch configurations are included: one that runs the tests and one that launches the extension development host and attaches to it.

➤ `settings.json`—Workspace-level settings file. For the scaffolded projects, it excludes the "out" folder from the search and file watching functionality.

➤ `tasks.json`—Defines the tasks for the project. In the scaffolded project, it defines a watch task as the default for the build group.

Next you see `node_modules` and `out` folders in the project. The `node_modules` folder contains the packages that are being used by the application. It's a standard folder for web applications, and the contents are typically determined by entries in the `package.json` file. The `out` folder is the place where output from the project's build process will be placed.

The `src` file is the implementation of the extension; not just the functionality, but also the tests that are written. The `test` folder contains the code related to running the tests. The scaffolded project contains some dummy tests, so that there is something that runs. But there is nothing in that code that actually tests any of the extension functionality.

The `extension.ts` file contains the implementation for the extension. Just to be clear, there is no requirement that the file be called `extension.ts`. That's just what the scaffolding has set up. It's the contents of the `extension.ts` that wires up the functionality, regardless of the name of the file in which it resides.

The remaining files fit into the category of configuration and documentation:

➤ `.gitignore`—Defines the collection of files and folders that are ignored by Git.

➤ `.vscodeignore`—Defines that collection of files that are intended to be ignored when the extension is installed.

➤ `CHANGELOG.md`—A Markdown file that documents the changes that are made to the extension from version to version.

➤ `package-lock.json`—An automatically generated file that contains the exact tree that was generated by an npm operation. The goal of the file is to define a single representation of the dependency tree generated by the installation of various packages.

➤ `package.json`—Part of the Node.js runtime environment, it includes all of the packages used by the application, including their versions. In addition, it has a number of optional attributes that are used at build time to contribute to the building process.

➤ `README.md`—A Markdown file that is a brief (or not) description of the functionality of the extension.

➤ `tsconfig.json`—The TypeScript configuration file.

➤ `tslint.json`—The configuration file for the TSLint extension. This file is only present if you have installed the recommended TSLint extension.

➤ `vsc-extension-quickstart.md`—A Markdown file that describes the contents of the scaffold project.

Now that the structure of the extension code has been covered, along with the basic flow of functionality through the extension, let's spend the next couple of sections diving into the different areas of extensibility that Visual Studio Code offers.

ACTIVATION EVENTS

When an extension is installed, it lets Visual Studio Code know that it is interested in any of a number of different events. When these events occur, at any point, Visual Studio Code activates the extension. This allows the extension to "wake up" and do whatever it was coded to do. The events that an extension can express an interest in are called activation events.

The activation events that a particular extension cares about are defined in the `package.json` file. They are part of the `activationEvents` attribute, which is an array of strings. The content of the string indicates the activation event and some additional qualifying information for the event.

The set of possible activation events is not particularly long, but the range of extensibility that can come from these events is much greater than you might think. The following sections discuss the different activation events and when they get triggered, along with what any additional qualifiers might look like.

onCommand

This activation was also discussed while looking at the sample extension. In this case, the activation event is raised when a command is executed. The qualifier is the full name of the command. The configuration would look like the following:

```
"activationEvents": [
    "onCommand: extension.helloWorld"
]
```

While all of the examples you see online use "extension. . ." in the code, that is truly just an example. You should be replacing *extension* with the identifier for your extension. So a more likely configuration would look like the following:

```
"activationEvents": [
    "onCommand: how-long.helloWorld"
]
```

Also, like the `onLanguage` extension, there is no limit to having a single `onCommand` act as the activation event.

onDebug

The `onDebug` activation event is raised just before a debug session is started. There is no qualifier, so the configuration looks like the following:

```
"activationEvents": [
    "onDebug"
]
```

The `onDebug` activation event might not be as granular as you need it to be, so two additional activation events are associated with debugging:

➤ `onDebugInitialConfiguration`—Raised just before the `DebugConfigurationProvider` is requested for its configuration information.

➤ `onDebugResolve:type`–Raised just before the `DebugConfigurationProvider` is requested to resolve the debug configuration.

To understand the process involved, it helps to understand how debuggers are specified and how the configuration for a debug session is constructed.

To start, debuggers are extensions. As such, they are constructed with their own `package.json` file. A `debuggers` attribute in the `contributes` section of that same file defines information about the debugger. See "Debuggers" in the "Contribution Points" section later in this chapter for information.

Now when a configuration is added to a `launch.json` file (see the Launch Configuration section in Chapter 6, "Debugging Your Code"), the extension is asked for the configuration that is used to create the array element added in `launch.json` file. The `onDebugInitialConfiguration` event is raised before the debugger extension is queried for its initial configuration.

When a debugging session is launched, there might be changes made to the debug configuration based on the session. The configuration that is in `launch.json` might be modified (say, for example, by resolving paths). This modification takes place by asking the debugger extension to resolve the configuration. The `onDebugResolve` event is triggered when this step takes place.

While it is definitely easier to just use the `onDebug` event, there are ramifications if the activation process does not happen quickly enough. Keep in mind that the debug session won't begin until the `onDebug` events are finished—and that the developer is waiting (not necessarily patiently) for that to happen. So if your extension appears to be sluggish when launching, it might be worth it to consider using one of the other two activation events for your extension.

onFileSystem

This activation event might seem a little odd, but it gets triggered based on the scheme that is used to retrieve a particular file or folder. Keep in mind that the typical scheme for opening a file or folder is `file://`, but you can access files using different protocols. A typical configuration might look like the following:

```
"activationEvents": [
    "onFileSystem: ftp"
]
```

This could cause the activation event to be raised if a file is retrieved using an `ftp://` link.

onLanguage

The `onLanguage` activation event is triggered whenever a file of a particular type is opened. The configuration would look like the following:

```
"activationEvents": [
    "onLanguage:javascript"
]
```

The qualifier in this case is the name of the language. It must be one of the valid language identifiers for Visual Studio Code. This is a list of around forty or so strings that are directly associated with known language. They range from BAT files to GO to Python and JavaScript, Java, and C#, as well as many languages you might not have thought of. You can find a list at `https://code.visualstudio.com/docs/languages/identifiers`.

There is also no reason to be limited to a single language. You can add additional languages by adding additional strings to the array, as in the following:

```
"activationEvents": [
    "onLanguage:javascript",
    "onLanguage:typescript"
]
```

onUri

This activation event allows an extension to be activated when a system-wide URI is opened. The configuration is pretty straightforward:

```
"activationEvents": [
    "onUri"
]
```

but the workings are a little more complex.

First, the activation event depends on whether a URI of a specific format is opened; the URI scheme is either *vscode* or *vscode-insiders*. Next, the URI authority must be the identity for the extension, so URIs would take the form of the following:

```
vscode://how-long/init
vscode-insiders://how-long/start?t=1033
```

After the scheme and authority have been provided, the remainder of the URI is arbitrary. It's up to the extension to process it. In other words, it will be up to the extension to recognize that (for example) `init` is in the URI and that means that the extension needs to be set to an initial state. Or (again, for example) to see the `start` in the URI and extract the query string parameter (`t=1033`).

In order to be passed the URI so that it can be processed, the extension calls `vscode.window.registerUrlHandler`. This registers the extension's interest in the URI with Visual Studio Code.

onView

The `onView` activation event works in conjunction with a view that has been added by an extension. The configuration looks like the following:

```
"activationEvents": [
    "onView: outstandingTasks"
]
```

Going strictly by the definition, what this means is that the `onView` activation event is triggered when the `outstandingTasks` view is opened. However, it says nothing about when that might happen. The answer is when your extension contributes a View Container and Tree Views to Visual Studio Code.

In order to do that, your extension defines a View Container in the `contributes` section of `package.json`, and then it would define one or more views that go inside that view container. The name of the view that you're creating is the qualifier that is associated with the `onView` event. The following configuration shows this relationship:

```
"contributes": {
    "viewsContainers": {
        "activitybar": [
            {
                "id": "task-explorer",
                "title": "Task Explorer",
                "icon": "media/task.svg"
            }
        ]
    },
    "views": {
        "task-explorer": [
            {
                "id": "outstandingTasks",
                "name": "Outstanding Tasks",
                "when": "explorer"
            }
        ]
    }
}
```

onWebviewPanel

The premise of this activation event is that it gets raised when a web view of a particular type is displayed. To be a little more precise, it's raised when the web view is restored. That distinction is important to understanding the purpose of the activation event. The configuration is as follows:

```
"activationEvents": [
    "onWebviewPanel: taskPanel"
]
```

The important connection to make is that this activation event is not sufficient, on its own, to launch an extension. The reason is that this event is triggered when Visual Studio Code opens up, and the web view, which was visible when Visual Studio Code was closed, is restored. However, in order for the web view to have been visible when Visual Studio Code was closed, there must have been another activation event that activated the extension. What this activation event is for is to allow your extension to get back to its previous state without the developer needing to do anything.

The qualifier for the configuration (`taskPanel` in the example) is the name of a web view that is created by a call to `vscode.window.createWebviewPanel`.

workspaceContains

This activation event is triggered when a folder is opened and the folder contains at least one file that matches the glob pattern that is the qualifier in the configuration. Consider the following:

```
"activationEvents": [
    "workspaceContains: **/.hlconfig"
]
```

Here the event is raised when the file `.hlconfig` is found someplace within the workspace that is opened.

Start Up

It is possible for an activation event to be raised when Visual Studio Code starts up. The configuration looks like the following:

```
"activationEvents": [
    "*"
]
```

While this is the easy way to ensure that your extension gets activated, it is not ideal. Visual Studio Code won't be available for the developer until all of the extensions that are listening to the `startup` event have been started. If every extension just activated on startup, you can imagine that performance might be negatively impacted. So consider carefully your other options before using the `startup` event.

CONTRIBUTION POINTS

The contribution points within Visual Studio Code are the places where extensions can add new functionality. In the following sections, the different places where Visual Studio Code has hooks for extensibility are described. Because this area is so rich, it's not possible to cover every possible combination. Instead, the sections will focus on discussing the underlying concepts and, where appropriate, how different pieces fit together.

The configuration for contribution points all takes place within the `contributes` section of the `package.json` file. For example, a command might look like the following:

```
"contributes": {
    "commands": [{
        "command": "how-long.helloWorld",
        "title": "Hello World",
        "category": "Greetings"
    }]
}
```

Notice that `contributes` in the preceding code is a JSON object, and `commands` is just a property within that object. The same is true for each contribution point. So, in this section, when we're discussing the configuration for a specific contribution point, only the property name will be shown. Presume that it's part of the `contributes` JSON object unless the text says something different.

breakpoints

The `breakpoints` contribution is only found in debugger extensions. It allows the extension to define the file types for which breakpoints are allowed. The contribution value itself is an array of JSON objects, where each one defines the language or file type:

```
"breakpoints": [
    {
        "language": "javascript"
    },
    {
        "language": "typescript"
    }
]
```

colors

As sad as you might be to hear this, you're not actually defining a new color with this contribution. What you're doing is mapping a color that is used in the extension to a color value that the user can control. Consider it like the following. Your extension is going to highlight the text anytime a particular keyword appears. You're defining the name of the setting from which you will take that color. The following is an example:

```
"colors": [{
    "id": "how-long.keywordHighlight",
    "description": "Color used to highlight the keywords.",
    "defaults": {
        "dark": "errorForeground",
        "light": "errorForeground",
        "highContrast": "#010203"
    }
}]
```

First off, notice that the `colors` contribution is an array of color objects. That is because an extension can define more than one color mapping. The idea is that the extension would use the `vscode.workspace.getConfiguration` method to get the color for a specific purpose from the configuration, and then use that color within the extension.

The `id` attribute is used to uniquely identify the color, and the `description` should give the developer an idea of how the color will be used in the extension. The `defaults` attribute describes the default colors in the absence of any changes by the developer. There are three separate defaults: one for dark themes, one for light themes, and one for high-contrast themes. The keyword used for the `dark` and `light` values in the sample reference colors that are part of the Visual Studio Code color palette.

configuration

This contribution point allows an extension to define a collection of properties that make up the configuration for the extension. What is really being contributed is a JSON schema that is then used to render the user interface found in the user and workspace settings. The following is an example of a `configuration` contribution:

```
"configuration": {
    "type": "object",
    "title": "How Long configuration",
    "properties": {
        "how-long.use24Hour": {
            "type": "boolean",
            "default": false,
            "description": "Time is represented using a 24-hour clock."
        },
    }
}
```

The `type` attribute is either an intrinsic data type (such as Boolean) or the literal object if this configuration has additional properties. It's possible to have multiple types for a single property. For example, the following allows the configuration value to be either a string or null:

```
...
    "type": ["string","null"],
...
```

It's also possible to create a configuration that contains an array of values:

```
"type": ["string", "array"],
"items": {
    "type": "string"
},
```

Or to force the user to select from a list:

```
"type": ["string"],
"enum": [
    "Ready",
    "In Progress",
    "Completed"
]
```

The values for the configuration can be read using the `vscode.workspace.getConfiguration` method.

configurationDefaults

In this case, the configuration defaults are not related to the configuration for the extension. Instead, the goal of this extension point is to change the default settings for a particular language. The following would change the default for JavaScript:

```
"configurationDefaults": {
    "[javascript]": {
        "editor.quickSuggestions": false
    }
}
```

Typically, the reason for wanting to modify the defaults for a language would be because the default behavior is conflicting with the extension's functionality in some way.

commands

The configuration for `commands` was discussed earlier in this chapter. This contribution adds a title, along with a command to be executed, to the Command Palette:

```
"commands": [{
    "command": "how-long.helloWorld",
    "title": "Hello World",
    "category": "Greeting"
}]
```

Optionally, you can include a category with the command. The category is prepended to the title in the Command Palette. This allows commands to be more conveniently grouped together.

debuggers

Contributing a debugger to Visual Studio Code is a bigger task than most other contributions. The reason is that it needs to have a separate executable that implements the debug protocol supported by Visual Studio Code. The contribution defines a reference to that executable and provides the schema that is required in `launch.json` in order to properly configure the debugger. A detailed description of how to contribute a debugger is well beyond the scope of this book, but you can find a detailed starting point at `https://code.visualstudio.com/api/extension-guides/debugger-extension`.

grammars

Visual Studio Code uses TextMate grammars in order to break content into a collection of tokens. TextMate is basically a specialized and structured collection of regular expressions. You can find more information about TextMate grammars at `https://macromates.com/manual/en/language_grammars`.

When you are contributing a grammar to Visual Studio Code, three elements are involved: the language, the top-level scope, and a path to the grammar file. The following is an example:

```
"grammars": [
    {
        "language": "mylua",
        "scopeName": "source.lua",
        "path": "./syntaxes/lua.icdGrammar.json"
    }
]
```

The example presumes that a language named mylua has been defined. See the "Languages" section for how this would be done. The top-level scope is `source.lua`. This matches the name of a scope found in the grammar file, the path to which is identified in the `path` attribute.

jsonValidation

The purpose of the `jsonValidation` contribution is to provide a link between a file pattern and a JSON schema:

```
"jsonValidation": [{
    "fileMatch": ".jshintrc",
    "url": "http://json.schemastore.org/jshintrc"
}]
```

The `fileMatch` attribute is used to determine which files need to be validated using the schema. The `url` attribute is a link to the schema itself. It can be either a local path to a schema provided in the extension, or available through a different protocol (like HTTP or HTTPS).

keybindings

A key binding is a rule that defines which command should be executed when a particular keyboard combination is pressed. If you contribute a key binding, it becomes part of the default keyboard shortcuts within Visual Studio Code, and if your command is represented in the UI (such as being seen in the list in Command Palette), the shortcut is displayed. The following is a simple key binding contribution:

```
"keybindings": [{
    "command": "extension.sayHello",
    "key": "ctrl+f1",
    "mac": "cmd+f1",
    "when": "editorTextFocus"
}]
```

The key binding can work in conjunction with the command contribution. The `command` attribute references a command. That command could be an existing command within Visual Studio Code or a command that your extension has contributed. In the latter case, the value of the `command` attribute must match the command being contributed.

The `key` attribute defines the keyboard combination that is used to trigger the command. Similar attributes are `mac`, `linux`, and `windows`. Each of those attributes is used to define the keyboard combination specific to those platforms. In the preceding example, both Linux and Windows would have used a keyboard combination of Ctrl+F1, while on macOS, the keyboard combination of Cmd+F1 would be used.

The `when` attribute is used to provide a granular means to identify when the key binding should be active. The expression evaluates to a Boolean value and when that value is true, the keyboard combination will work.

when Clause

The premise of the `when` clause is that Visual Studio Code surfaces variables that are being updated based on the user's actions. These changes cause your menu to be enabled or disabled. The surfaced variables are quite granular; they range from identifying your operating environment (`isLinux`, `isMac`, `isWindows`) to whether an editor has focus (`editorFocus`, `editorTextFocus`) or that something in the editor has been selected (`editorHasSelections`). You can find a complete list of the different variables at `https://code.visualstudio.com/docs/getstarted/keybindings#_when-clause-contexts`.

The when clause can combine these variables using simple logical operators. The AND (&&), OR (‖), and NOT (!) operators are all valid, as well as checks for equality (==). As an example, the following checks that the platform is Windows and that the editor has focus:

```
isWindows && editorFocus
```

Some of the variables have values rather than providing a Boolean flag. For instance, the following checks to see if the editor is working with a file associated with JavaScript:

```
resourceLangId == 'javascript'
```

languages

A languages contribution is an interesting combination of simple and complex. The simple is pretty straightforward:

```
"languages": [{
    "id": "mylua",
    "extensions": [ ".mylua" ],
    "aliases": [ "MyLua", "ml" ],
    "filenames": [ "**/.mlua" ],
    "firstLine": "^#!/.*\\bmylua[0-9.-]*\\b",
    "configuration": "./language-configuration.json"
}]
```

The id attribute is the identifier for the language, expected to be used elsewhere in Visual Studio Code. The extensions array is a list of the filename extensions that are used to link a file to this language automatically. The filenames array, like extensions, is used to specify filename patterns that should be considered as being written in the language. The aliases extension is a list of user-friendly names for this language. Even the firstLine attribute is used, by allowing you to specify a regular expression that is used to identify files for this language by matching the first line in the text to the expression.

Where it gets more complicated is in the configuration attribute. This value points to a language configuration file that defines a set of declarative features about the language: things like the characters used to indicate comments, the pairs of automatically closing brackets, and patterns that indicate when groups of lines can be folded. This configuration doesn't have anything to do with the language grammar (that is defined in the grammars contribution), but instead is how the editor interacts with the text in the files. For more details about the language configuration file, check out https://code.visualstudio.com/api/language-extensions/language-configuration-guide.

menus

The menus configuration works in conjunction with a command. In fact, there has to be a related command for the menus contribution to work. Let's work with the following sample configuration:

```
"menus": {
    "editor/context": [{
        "when": "editorTextFocus",
        "command": "how-long.startTimer",
        "alt": "how-long.stopTimer",
        "group": "navigation"
    }]
}
```

The starting point is one of the menus to which contributions are allowed by Visual Studio Code. The menu corresponds to the name of the attribute. The list of available menus follows:

➤ *commandPalette*—The Command Palette.

➤ *explorer/context*—The context menu associated with the Explorer view.

➤ *editor/context*—The context menu associated with the editor.

➤ *editor/title*—The menu bar that appears in the editor title.

➤ *editor/title/context*—The context menu that appears when the editor title is right-clicked.

➤ *debug/callstack/context*—The context menu for the Callstack view visible while debugging.

➤ *debug/toolbar*—The toolbar visible when in a debug session.

➤ *scm/title*—The title menu for the source control manager.

➤ *scm/resourceGroup/context*—The source control manager resource groups menu.

➤ *scm/resource/context*—The menu for the source control manager's resources.

➤ *scm/change/title*—The title bar of an inline change.

➤ *view/title*—The title menu of a view.

➤ *view/item/context*—The context menu for an item within a view.

➤ *touchBar*—The Touch Bar in macOS.

Each one of these attributes is actually an array of menu commands. Each menu command has up to four attributes:

➤ command—The name of the command that will be executed. This command needs to have a corresponding entry in the commands contribution, since it provides the name that is displayed for this menu item.

➤ alt—The name of the command that is executed when the Alt key is pressed at the same time as the menu item.

➤ group—The group to which this menu item belongs. The group is used to sort related menu items together. The exception is if you specify the group "navigation." This group causes the menu item to appear at the top of the list.

➤ when—This attribute defines the criteria for when the menu item is activated. This is an expression that evaluates to a Boolean value. When the expression is true, the menu item is available to be used.

One thing you might question is why one of the potential menu targets is the Command Palette. After all, the commands contribution is capable of adding a command to the palette. But the rationale has to do with the when clause. If you target the Command Palette and include a when clause, you are restricting when the command might be available, functionality that the commands contribution doesn't offer on its own.

problemMatchers

The goal of a problem matcher in Visual Studio Code is to provide a mechanism for adding meaning-ful information to the Problems pane. For example, if you have a file that is transpiled as part of the build process and an error is detected, you might see a message like the following:

```
sample.mylua: 35:15 Unrecognized method name.
```

A problem matcher would take this output, parse out the meaningful pieces, and add a message to the Problems pane:

```
"problemMatchers": [
    {
        "name": "ml-build",
        "owner": "mylua",
        "fileLocation": ["relative", "${workspaceFolder}"],
        "pattern": {
            "regexp": "^(.*):(\\d+):(\\d+):\\s+(.*)$",
            "file": 1,
            "line": 2,
            "column": 3,
            "message": 4
        }
    }
]
```

The `name` of the problem matcher is the identifier. The `owner` indicates the language that is associ-ated with the problem. The `fileLocation` is used to identify where the output that is being matched against the pattern can be found. Finally, there is the `pattern` itself.

The pattern consists of a regular expression that is matched against each of the lines in the output file. If the line matches the pattern, the values from the expression are captured and assigned to `file`, `line`, `column`, and `message`. These values are used to add an entry to the Problems pane. The nice thing is that by capturing values like `file` and `line`, it becomes possible for the developer to double-click a line in the Problems pane and have the appropriate file opened and the cursor positioned to the error location.

snippets

The `snippets` contribution is used to identify a file containing snippets that are to be added by the extension. The format for the snippets file is the same as for user-defined snippets. You can find a description at `https://code.visualstudio.com/docs/editor/userdefinedsnippets#_snip-pet-syntax`.

As for the contribution itself, here's an example:

```
"snippets": [{
    "language": "mylua",
    "path": "./snippets/mylua.json"
}]
```

The `language` attribute references a language with which these snippets are to be associated, and the `path` attribute is the path to the JSON file that contains the snippet definitions.

taskDefinitions

The `taskDefinition` contribution defines a schema for a task that is being contributed by the extension. The definition includes the type of the task with which the schema is being associated, the list of properties in the schema, and the properties that are required (as opposed to being optional). Within each property, there is a data type and an associated description:

```
"taskDefinitions": [
    {
        "type": "npm",
        "required": [
            "script"
        ],
        "properties": {
            "script": {
                "type": "string",
                "description": "The script to execute"
            },
            "path": {
                "type": "string",
                "description": "The path to the package.json file. If omitted the
package.json in the root of the workspace folder is used."
            }
        }
    }
]
```

This contribution is for a task that opens the `package.json` file, locates a script with the given name, and executes it. Keep in mind that the task definition is not about actually performing this task. It is about defining what goes into the `task.json` file so that another process can perform the task.

themes

This contribution is used to add a TextMate theme to Visual Studio Code:

```
"themes": [{
    "label": "Vanessence",
    "uiTheme": "vs-dark",
    "path": "./themes/Vanessence.tmTheme"
}]
```

The `label` attribute is the user-friendly name to be displayed when selecting a theme. The `uiTheme` value indicates whether it is considered to be a light, dark, or high-contrast theme. That distinction can impact different colors in different parts of Visual Studio Code (see the `colors` contribution for an idea of how that works). Finally, the `path` indicates the TextMate theme file. You can read up on how to create that theme file at https://code.visualstudio.com/api/extension-guides/color-theme.

viewsContainers

A view container is a container that holds different views. While accurate, that definition is not really helpful without a bit more context.

In Visual Studio Code, View Containers are activated by clicking an icon in the Activity Bar. The Explorer is a View Container, as is the Source Control. What's not obvious is that the contents of Explorer and Source Control are actually views. So the view container is the relationship between the activity bar icon and a UI element that displays a collection of views.

This relationship is contributed by the following JSON:

```
"viewsContainers": {
    "activitybar": [
        {
            "id": "how-long-explorer",
            "title": "How Long Items",
            "icon": "resources/how-long-explorer.svg"
        }
    ]
}
```

Inside the `viewsContainers` element is an `activitybar` attribute. That attribute is an array of view containers. The premise is that you specify the target for the icon, and then the icon itself. So here you have added a view container with a title of "How Long Items" and the specified icon. This icon will appear at the bottom of the activity bar.

While this structure might suggest that there are more places where you can put a view container icon, at the moment, the only target is the activity bar. The look of the icon is pretty specifically dictated: it should be 28×28 pixels and centered on a 50×40 block, and it should also be monochromatic so as not to significantly alter the look of Visual Studio Code.

views

The view is the second part of the view container relationship. When you contribute a view, you designate where your view will be placed and when it might be considered active. But the contribution just sets up the relationship. The rendering of the view is triggered by an `onView` activation event that was covered in the "Activation Events" section:

```
"views": {
    "how-long-explorer": [
        {
            "id": "workItemList",
            "name": "Open Work Items",
            "when": "workspaceHasPackageJSON"
        }
    ]
}
```

In this example, a view called `workItemList` is added to the View Container defined in the `viewsContainers` example. Along with any custom view containers the extension might add, you can target four intrinsic view containers: explorer, scm (Source Control), debug, and test.

When the view container that is the host for this view is opened, the `onView` activation event is raised with the `id` value included as a qualifier. It would then be up to the extension to react to that event by rendering the contents of the view.

VISUAL STUDIO CODE API

You have already seen a couple of examples of the Visual Studio Code API in this chapter, mostly related to being able to retrieve the current configuration for situations where the developer is able to modify default settings. But there are certainly a lot more areas where useful functionality is available.

Basically, the Visual Studio Code API is a set of JavaScript APIs that you can use to access and manipulate parts of Visual Studio Code. In this section, we look at the different namespaces that are exposed. Not every single method will be covered in detail (it is a very extensive and evolving API), but the ones that are most likely to be useful to extension writers will be.

Common Patterns

Since the API is based on JavaScript, a number of patterns used are common not only across the APIs, but within JavaScript. To avoid questioning the why and how of some of the calls, it's worth drilling into the JavaScript concepts before getting started.

Promises

In order to avoid taking out a dependency on any Promise library, the Visual Studio Code API uses a *Thenable* type. The Thenable type represents the lowest common denominator across all promise libraries: then. The then method takes up to two parameters. The first is a function that is invoked when the promise is resolved, and the second is a function that is invoked when the promise is rejected.

In most cases, the use of Promises is optional. The API calls are capable of supporting the user of the Thenable pattern or just the actual return value.

Cancellation Tokens

In some instances API calls are made during situations where the state at the time of the invocation is changeable. That seems like an odd scenario for many developers, but consider a situation where the API is called to retrieve the list of methods in an IntelliSense context. While the API is collecting the list, the user keeps typing, making the returned list obsolete.

APIs that expose this type of behavior are passed a cancellation token. This allows the API to check on the current state of the request and whether processing needs to continue, based on the isCancellationRequested property.

Events

In the Visual Studio Code API, events are exposed as functions to which you can subscribe. The basic flow is create listener function, associate listener with event, dispose of the association when finished. The following code shows an example:

```
var listener = function(event) {
  console.log('Here I am', event);
};

var subscription = fsWatcher.onWillDelete(listener);

...

subscription.dispose();
```

The pattern of the event names is consistent throughout the API. They look like on[Will|Did]Verb. The *Will* version of the event is triggered before the verb takes place. The *Did* version of the event is raised after the verb.

Commands

A command is a function with a unique identifier that can be triggered either through the Command Palette or through a user interface gesture, like keyboard binding.

Within the API, you need to register a command by specifying the name of the command and the function that gets invoked when the command is triggered:

```
commands.registerCommand('how-long.startWorking', () => {
    window.showInformationMessage('Gettings started');
});
```

Here, the command is how-long.startWorking and the function that is invoked when the developer executes that command is defined in the anonymous function passed as the second parameter.

You can also register a text editor command using the registerTextEditorCommand method. The difference is that the callback function is passed a reference to the current TextEditor and Text-EditorEdit objects. These references allow you to get and modify the current state of the text editor. As a result, registered text editor commands are only available to be executed while there is an active text editor.

There are also methods that allow you to execute an arbitrary command (executeCommand) or get a list of commands (getCommands).

Debug

A number of functions are available to query and modify the debug state. But because debugging is typically handled in a debugger extension, the exposed functionality might seem relatively limited. Figure that most extensions aren't going to have direct access to debugging functionality unless they are actually debuggers.

As a result, the API exposes as properties a list of breakpoints, and references to the active Debug Console and debug session.

Exposed methods include the ability to add and remove breakpoints and to start a debugging session. To help support these functions, the API also raises events when the breakpoint list has been changed, and the debugging session initiated or terminated.

Env

The Env namespace contains properties that describe the current executing environment. This includes the name of the application, the root folder in which the application is running, the current language, the unique identifier for the machine, and an identifier for the current session.

An interesting value that can be retrieved through this namespace is the clipboard. This means you can have access to copy and paste items using your extension that have been added to the clipboard from outside your extensions.

Also, there is a method called openExternal that takes a URI as a parameter and opens that item using the default application. So an HTTP URI would be opened by a browser, or a MAILTO URI would be opened by a mail application.

Extensions

This namespace allows an extension to access the API exposed by another extension. First, realize that any extension has the ability to expose an API surface. This is done by returning the surface from the activate method:

```
export function activate(context: vscode.ExtensionContext) {
    let api = {
        add(a, b) {
            return a + b;
        },
        multiply(a, b) {
            return a * b;
        }
    };

    return api;
}
```

In this case, the extension has two methods that can be accessed by other extensions: add and multiply.

For this API to be accessed in an extension, you could use the following code:

```
let myExt = extensions.getExtension('how-log.calculations');
let api = myExt.exports;

console.log(api.multiply(6, 9));
```

Languages

If it hasn't been obvious, there are a lot of different languages out there. Many have support in Visual Studio Code, either natively or through extensions. But a lot of different syntaxes and semantics are scattered through the different languages.

Most people working with any language want autocompletion, code navigation, and static code checking. To facilitate this, the UI elements for all of these features are built into Visual Studio Code. So from a language perspective, what you need to do is provide the data.

The namespace includes methods like:

➤ registerCodeLensProvider—Registers the provider of data for the code lens functionality.

➤ registerDocumentHighlightProvider—Registers the provider that determines whether part of a document should be highlighted.

➤ registerDocumentSymbolProvider—Registers the provider that contains the symbols for the document. This would be used for the Go To Symbol functionality.

➤ registerRenameProvider—Registers the provider that provides rename functionality.

Scm

The scm namespace has a single method in it: `createSourceControl`. It takes an identifier for the source control to be created and returns an instance of the `SourceControl` object. Through that object, you have access to properties like the commands found in the Status Bar and the input box that is found within the Source Control view.

Tasks

Through the tasks namespace, you can perform functions on the tasks defined in the `tasks.json` file. This includes getting a list of tasks, getting a list of the tasks that are currently being executed, and starting a particular task. Events that are supported include being notified when tasks begin and end.

Window

This namespace is used to deal with the current window of the Visual Studio Code. It contains references to the terminals (including the active terminal) and the active text editor. Each of those references returns objects (`terminal` and `textEditor`) through which an extension can access and modify the underlying user-interface elements. The exposed events are raised when the terminals and text editors are changed (not the contents, but when the user selected a different terminal, for example).

But for most extensions, the big functionality offered by this namespace is access to various display and input elements. For example:

```
vscode.window
  .showInformationMessage('What\'s Next', 'first', 'second', 'third')
  .then(choice => {
    console.log(choice);
  });
```

This will display a message `What's Next`, along with three choices (`first`, `second`, and `third`). The value that the user selects will be passed in as the `choice` parameter to the `then` function.

Some of the methods are:

➤ `createStatusBarItem`—Creates a Status Bar item. The returned value is a `StatusBarItem` that allows the extension to display messages or to have the item execute a command when clicked.

➤ `createTreeView`—Creates a tree view for a view. The idea is that the extension has a previously defined view as one of its contributions. And that view contains a set of data. This method creates a tree view that is a representation of the data.

➤ `createWebviewPanel`—Creates and displays a new Webview panel.

➤ `registerTreeDataProvider`—Registers a `TreeDataProvider` with a contributed view. This allows the view that is displayed when a view container is opened to be populated with data.

➤ `setStatusBarMessage`—Displays a message on the Status Bar.

➤ `showErrorMessage`—Displays an error message.

➤ showInformationMessage—Displays an information message.

➤ showInputBox—Displays a text box that is used to capture user input. The value returned by this method is the text input by the user.

➤ showOpenDialog—Displays the File Open dialog. The method is Thenable, with the URI for the selected file passed as a parameter.

➤ showQuickPick—Displays a list of items and allows the user to select one or more. The method is Thenable, with the selected item passed as a parameter to the callback function.

➤ showSaveDialog—Displays the File Save dialog.

➤ showTextDocument—Opens a document using the associated editor.

➤ showWarningMessage—Displays a warning message.

Workspace

This namespace is a combination of two main elements. First, a number of objects and methods are associated with the current workspace. Second, the namespace includes methods and properties that are used to work with the current workspace, including all of the files and folders. There is a method to create a file system watcher (createFileSystemWatcher), which raises an event when a file is modified, and there is a method to search through the files in the workspace (findFiles) used. Both of these methods are executed out of the editor process, so they are quite performant—more so than if you were to use the native Node.js methods for the same functionality.

Aside from those methods (and a few more), the Workspace namespace contains the declarations for many of the other objects used within the Visual Studio Code API. From CancellationToken to Clipboard, Command to Task, the various JavaScript objects needed to interact with the API are in this workspace.

SUMMARY

The breadth and depth of extensibility for Visual Studio Code is impressive. Because the application was designed to be extensible, it's not surprising that what you can do and how you can tie your extension into the application means that almost anything you can envision is possible.

INDEX